The Impact of the Social Sciences

The Impact of the
Social Sciences

By Kenneth E. Boulding

Rutgers University Press

New Brunswick, New Jersey

Third Printing

Copyright © 1966 by Rutgers, The State University
Library of Congress Catalogue Number: 66-64653
ISBN: 0-8135-0525-9
Printed in the United States of America

✸✸✸✸   **Preface**

These chapters originated in the Brown and Haley Lectures at the University of Puget Sound, March 29–31, 1966. I have taken the liberty of expanding the substance of the lectures somewhat for the purposes of this volume. The first two chapters contain the substance of the first lecture, the third chapter the second lecture, and the fourth chapter the third lecture. The fifth chapter is by way of an epilogue.

If a certain air of possibly unwarranted optimism pervades these chapters, it must be blamed on the view of Mount Rainier, the wonderful feeling of early spring in the Northwest, and the warm hospitality and stimulating discussions which I enjoyed at the College of Puget Sound. I hope this little volume will carry something of the atmosphere of the visiting lectureship. Is is in no sense definitive or exhaustive. It is neither a treatise nor a textbook. But I hope that it will at least raise a few hares that will prove to be chaseable.

Kenneth E. Boulding

Ann Arbor, Michigan
May, 1966

✺✺✺✺ **Contents**

The 1966 Brown and Haley Lectures are the fourteenth of a series that has been given annually at the University of Puget Sound, Tacoma, Washington, by a scholar distinguished for his work in the Social Studies or the Humanities. The purpose of these lectures is to present original analyses of some intellectual problems confronting the present age.

The Impact of the Social Sciences

1

The Social Sciences and the Social System

The social system consists of all human beings on the planet and all their interrelationships, such as kinship, friendship, hostility, status, exchange, money flows, conversation, information outputs and inputs, and so on. It includes likewise the contents of every person's mind and the physical surroundings, both natural and artificial, to which he relates. This social system clings to the surface of the earth, so that it may appropriately be called the sociosphere, even though small fragments of it are now going out into space. The sociosphere thus takes its place with the lithosphere, the hydrosphere, the atmosphere, the biosphere, and so on as one of the systems which enwrap this little globe. It has strong interrelations with the other spheres with which it is mingled and without which it could not survive. Nevertheless, it has a dynamic and an integrity of its own. It is rather thin in Antarctica, although present there; it is very dense in New York. It is a network rather than a solid sphere or shell, yet no part of the earth's surface is very far from it. It is a system of enormous complexity, yet not wholly beyond our comprehension.

An essential part of the sociosphere and one of the major determinants of its dynamic course is man's knowledge of it—that is, of himself and of his society. It is only within the last two hundred years and in a sense almost within this generation that man has become widely conscious of his own societies and of the larger sociosphere of which they are a part. This movement of the social system into self-consciousness is perhaps one of the most significant phenomena of our time, and it represents a very fundamental break with the past, as did the development of personal self-consciousness many millennia earlier.

Without self-consciousness the dynamics of any evolutionary system is one of random mutation and selection. This is inevitably a very slow process, simply because any system as it exists at the moment has obviously been selected for survival, and therefore most variations away from it are likely not to survive. With the development of self-consciousness in man, the evolutionary process became at least in part teleological, that is, directed by an image of the future in the minds of active participants who were capable of affecting the system. With the development of self-consciousness a major learning process began in the human species, a learning process, moreover, of a cumulative nature, which could survive the death of the individual and be transmitted to the next generation. It is this cumulative increase of knowledge which constitutes the essence of the developmental process.

Knowledge in the broad sense of information structures and improbable arrangements of things is the key to the whole evolutionary process from hydrogen, the simplest element, on. It is, indeed, the only thing that is capable of evolution, for matter and energy taken together are conserved. In fact, the situation is even worse than that; matter and energy are not really conserved, but by the second law of thermodynamics available energy is dissipated, and every action exhausts some of the potential for further action. The dynamics of matter and energy, therefore, is a dynamics of devolution, not evolution. It is only information and knowledge which are capable of producing an evolutionary process of growth towards complexity and ultimately towards self-consciousness.

With the development of the self-conscious organism, that is man, the evolutionary process was able to proceed within his image and did not have to be confined to the phenomenal world. Hence man becomes an agent for creating the future which he imagines himself. The future is created first in the image by a process of evolution much more rapid than that which takes place outside, and then man gradually acquires the capability of realizing his image of the future as he achieves more knowledge and power.

Man's consciousness of himself produced tools, agriculture, and even civilization. It is only within the last two hundred years, however, that he has become conscious of his social system. Before that time he accepted the social system much as he accepted the seasons, the thunder and lightning, and the other natural phenomena around him, which he could observe but could not control. The rise of knowledge of social systems, however, has within it the seeds of their control, that is, the development of ideal images of the future within the minds of those who have the power to achieve them. There is something a little frightening about this; nevertheless it is the fruit of the tree of knowledge, and having eaten it we must put up with the consequences.

In any case we must recognize that knowledge about the social system is an essential part of it and that by affecting our behavior it affects the course of the social system itself. This is true even at the level of quite inexact or even superstitious knowledge. As we move towards more secure and exact knowledge of the social system the process of change is likely to accelerate. The rate of social invention is likely to increase, and in a relatively short time we may see profound transformations in social institutions and behavior as a result of cumulating knowledge about the system itself.

If we look at the rate of increase of the operating body of human knowledge as the key to development, it is clear that there have been at least three stages in this process, stages which, incidentally, still survive today. The first of these I call the "folk knowledge" process, which is the process by which we acquire knowledge in the ordinary business of life and ordinary relationships, in the family, among friends, in the peer group, and so on. This was almost the only knowledge process in the paleolithic era, and indeed up to the beginning of civilization. It is by no means ineffective in producing valid knowledge, especially of small and relatively simple systems. It was knowledge of this kind which enabled primitive man to survive and perpetuate himself. It suffers from the defect that it is hard to cumulate, for it is contained only in the heads of the living. In small societies especially it was easy for knowledge which might have been accumulated for some generations to be lost through an epidemic or disaster which killed off those who had the knowledge in their heads before it could be transmitted to the next generation, and the society would have to start all over again.

The Age of Civilization, from, say, 3000 B.C. to the present, is characterized by what might be called the literary knowledge process, involving the use of writing or other forms of recording knowledge. This makes the problem of transmission of the knowledge stock from one generation to the next much easier, permits more specialization in knowledge so that the knowledge stock is not confined to what a single head can hold, and also, provided the capacity to read can be transmitted, gives each generation access to information from the dead as well as from the living. This process permitted the formation of much more complex societies than orally transmitted folk knowledge could hope to produce and produced what might be called the classical civilizations.

Literary knowledge, however, is subject to certain defects that folk knowledge does not possess. In folk knowledge, within the limits of the simple systems with which it deals, error is quite rapidly detected because of the rapid feedback. If I mistake another lady for my wife and behave accordingly, I very soon find out and correct the error in my image, whether I live in a primitive or a developed society. Where the payoffs for error are negative and for truth are highly positive, a selective process against error takes place very rapidly.

Even in systems of folk knowledge, of course, superstition can arise in the case of systems where images may be self-fulfilled, where perception of error is difficult, and where images are received as true because of the authority of the teacher rather than through any testing process on the part of the learner. In the case of literary knowledge, the tendency towards superstition is even greater. The authority of the written word is profound, especially when it comes down from the remote past, and hence in a literate society it is quite possible that error is transmitted almost as easily as truth. Truth and error grow side by side, like the tares and the wheat.

The third knowledge process, which has been characteristic only of the last three hundred years, is the scientific process. The present enormously accelerated rate of change in the social system and in the condition of man is almost wholly due to a mutation in the method of acquiring and transmitting knowledge which took place three or four hundred years ago in western Europe, to which we give the name of science. The change took place within a very small subculture; it is almost a miracle, indeed, that it ever took place at all; and it is quite puzzling why it took place in Europe and not in China, which had been the most developed part of the world, certainly from the time of Christ until about 1600.

Whatever the explanation, the facts are not in dispute. From the sixteenth century on in Europe, we find a small but continuously growing group of people who specialize in the increase of knowledge by a method which involves the constant revision of images of the world under the impact of refined observation and testing. The origins of science, of course, go back a long way, certainly to Greece and Babylon. As a social movement in the acceleration of knowledge, however, it does not much antedate 1600, and the founding of the Royal Society in London in 1660 may perhaps be taken to symbolize the emergence of science as a legitimate and established subculture.

The increase in knowledge which this movement has generated has almost doubled the span of human life, has carried man into space, has explored the whole surface of the earth, has released enormous sources of energy, has created wholly new materials, and has created an enormous increase in productivity and affluence. It has increased per capita incomes in some parts of the world at least twenty times in two hundred years; it has also given us fantastic weapons, enormous insecurity in the international system, death-dealing modes of transport, an almost unmanageable population explosion, and the neurotic personality of our time. With all these costs, however, if most people today were offered the choice of living in the kind of developed society which the scientific revolution has produced and, shall we say, the merely civilized society of seventeenth-century London or first-century Rome, the choice, if realistic, would be pretty easy.

It should be emphasized that the processes by which images are created or mutate and the process by which error is weeded out and truth selected among these images is not essentially different in the three modes of acquisition of knowledge. If I want to go to the post office, I use folk language. I have been there before and I know my way. I do not use theodolites or any advanced scientific instrumentation; if it is my home town, I do not even have to use a map, which represents the literary level. If when I get to where I think the post office is I find it has been closed, my erroneous image is rapidly corrected, and by very simple folk processes of asking the bystanders I can usually find out where the post office in fact is now located. Then my image can be just as true as the most refined scientific image of the nucleus.

Literary knowledge, even though it is subject to what might be called authoritative superstition, is likewise subject to testing. If a road map has mistakes, complaints arise very rapidly and the mistakes are corrected. If following the recipe in a cookbook fails to produce the cake, again there will be rapid feedback to the publisher and the mistake will be corrected.

There are even payoffs to historians for discovering the mistakes of their predecessors.

Therefore the difference between folk and literary knowledge, on the one hand, and scientific knowledge, on the other, is not in their fundamental method of acquiring truth. The difference lies rather in the complexity of the systems that can be handled. The scientific process enables us to handle systems which are more complex than those that can be handled through folk knowledge or even ordinary literary means. We can find the post office by folk knowledge; we could find our way to California with a road map; but if we are going to be an astronaut we must have scientific knowledge, otherwise we will very soon be in deep trouble.

The reasons why the subculture of the scientists has been capable of acquiring reasonably true knowledge of very complex systems are twofold. In the first place, the scientific subculture has developed mathematical and logical inference from operational models. The process of logical and mathematical inference gives us predictions from the model which are very precise, whether they are unconditional, as in the case of the planets, or conditional, as in the case of a scientific experiment. From the mathematical model we predict that a planet will be at such and such a place in the heavens at such and such a time; we may also predict that if we do a, b, c, and d, e will follow, under exactly defined circumstances. The second reason for the success of science has been the development of refined instruments for observation and perception—the telescope, the microscope, the synchrotron, and, one might add, survey research and national income statistics.

Experiment, it should be noted, is not essential to the scientific process; prediction, however, in the sense of an exact image of the future, is essential. When the future is fulfilled the image of the present can be compared with the past image of the future, and if there is a divergence between the two something has to give. In the case of folk processes and even literary processes, it is all too easy either to reject the inference which gave rise to the prediction and to say that we shouldn't have made the prediction in the first place, or to reject the image of the present and say that things did not really turn out that way. In the scientific subculture we are protected against these reactions by logical inference on the one hand and careful instrumentation on the other; hence if there is disappointment there is no alternative but a fundamental revision of the basic model or image of the world. A failure of prediction is a sign of error, though success in prediction is not necessarily a sign of truth. The method of science, however, is essentially a mutation-selection process by which erroneous images are continually eliminated. The more error is eliminated, the more, one hopes, there is an asymptotic approach to truth.

The method of experiment, while it is not essential to science and is not a peculiar or distinguishing characteristic of it, nevertheless has been enormously important in the expansion of the scientific image of the universe. It involves the development of artificially simplified subsystems in which a relatively small number of variables can be identified and in which, therefore, it is easier to make exact predictions from the models. Even though it is enormously useful, the method of experiment likewise has its dangers. The subsystem that we use for our experiment may not be representative of the universe we are really trying to investigate, and the problem of the nature of the sample, therefore, becomes very important. Even the natural scientists are not entirely innocent of the charge of jumping to conclusions about the universe from very small samples of it that may not be wholly representative.

The division between the physical, biological, and social sciences corresponds roughly to three different kinds of systems in our environment of an increasing scale of complexity. Man as the knower himself participates in all three. He is a physico-chemical system in the physico-chemical environment, as he will find out very rapidly if he takes poison or jumps off the

Empire State Building. He is also a biological system of enormous complexity about which we still really understand very little. The mind boggles at the interaction of the ten billion neurons which constitute itself. As an individual, man also participates in a social system and in a sociosphere whose relations are not only enormously complex in themselves but, insofar as they are relations among humans, also participate in all the biological complexity of the human organism. The neuron which constitutes the essential element of the human nervous system is relatively simple compared with man himself, the individual person which constitutes the element of the social system.

In view of the enormous complexity of the sociosphere, it is certainly not unreasonable to ask the question, What are the limitations of the scientific method or of any other method for acquiring knowledge about social systems? Even some scientists have argued that the scientific method was not appropriate in the search for knowledge about social systems, perhaps because of the value systems involved, perhaps because of the fact that man himself and his knowledge is a part of the system which he studies. The question is not, however, whether the social sciences are "scientific"; this is just a semantic matter, for there is no single method of science applicable to all systems and all disciplines, and insofar as social systems and even biological systems are profoundly different in their nature from physical systems they will require different methods of inquiry. The crucial question is, What can we find out about social systems that is true?

We can perhaps be encouraged by the reflection that even a great deal of folk knowledge of social systems is at least true enough for the purposes of ordinary life. Indeed, when a person becomes incapable of testing the realities of his images of the social system in which he is personally placed, we tend to shut him up in a mental hospital. Most of us who are not so incarcerated operate in the social relations of our families, our jobs, and in various organizations to which we belong, in driving a car in a crowded street, in a public park, and so on, according to folk images which are at least true enough to keep us out of serious trouble.

The problem comes when we try to apply these folk images or even the literary images which are merely extended folk images to the social system as a whole in all its complexity. Then folk knowledge tends to break down and more refined methods of acquiring knowledge of social systems have to be developed. For the social equivalent of going to the post office, folk knowledge is fine; for the social equivalent of an astronautical expedition, it is quite inadequate and will lead to disaster. Therefore we must recognize that in dealing with complex social systems, and especially with social systems in the large, we must devise methods of acquiring knowledge and of testing our images which go beyond the processes of folk knowledge. Whether we call these methods "science" or not is beside the point. The real point is that we have to develop sophisticated methods in the acquisition and the testing of knowledge, and this is the major task of the social sciences.

Thus the social sciences will not teach us how to behave at a bridge party any more than we would use a theodolite to get to the post office. They are going to be helpful in training personnel managers and people who are responsible for large organizations, the dynamics of which go beyond their personal experience, even though in this connection a fairly literary type of knowledge is often quite adequate, as a flat road map is adequate in driving across the country. The management of a total economic system or an international system, however, is equivalent to the astronaut's journey. This requires methods for forming images, acquiring and processing information, testing predictions, and subsequently modifying the images which are far more elaborate than those which are adequate in the simpler systems. The case for the social sciences is simply the case for specialized, organized, knowledge-producing industries at the level of complex systems.

It is obviously impossible in the space of a relatively short volume to cover the whole field of the social sciences and their impact. In what follows, therefore, I have selected three areas, three subsystems as it were within the sociosphere, for more detailed analysis. The first is the economic system, or "econosphere," which is the sphere of all those relationships which are principally organized through exchange and the production and consumption of exchangeables. I have taken this as an example of the most sophisticated and elaborate body of social-scientific knowledge and that which has had the most profound effect on the sociosphere itself. Then I have selected the international system as that aspect of the sociosphere on which the social sciences have had the least impact and which is still operated largely by folk and literary knowledge in spite of the fact that it is a system of a degree of complexity which demands highly sophisticated knowledge processes. Then finally I propose to look at an aspect of the social life where the impact of the social sciences is at present very ambiguous, namely in the field of ethics, religion, and the law.

There are a good many aspects of social systems which I shall neglect or mention only in passing. For instance, the impact of anthropologists on the people they have investigated has often been profound. Hardly anything illustrates better the principle that knowledge is the key to development—positive or negative—than the impact of new knowledge on primitive societies. I have taken only passing notice of the impact of new knowledge on the family, perhaps because this is still an area in which folk knowledge is highly predominant in the governing of behavior. I have not taken more than a passing glance, either, at the impact of the social sciences on the educational system, which in a more exhaustive treatise would certainly demand a chapter to itself. I have also neglected the impact of social-scientific knowledge on internal political processes and on the structure and conduct of organizations. In a more complete work, the impact of the social sciences on architecture and constructions would also be considered, and the impact of medical practice. The list could be extended considerably. My object in this essay, however, is not to be exhaustive but to be illustrative and to point the way toward that larger and more systematic treatment of the theme which still lies in the future.

I suspect, indeed, that the story of the impact of the social sciences will not be written for five hundred years. It will take at least that long even for the implications of present knowledge to work themselves out. The last hundred years has seen an enormous impact of physics and chemistry on the economic system and all other aspects of social and political life. Whole new industries, new sources of energy, completely new occupations, and even a new image of man have resulted. We are only just beginning to see the impact of the biological sciences in the present generation, and it is quite likely that the next fifty years may be regarded as the flowering of the biological age in which man perhaps begins to manipulate the genetic process, develop new forms of life, and even break the aging barrier.

The full impact of the social sciences may not be felt for a hundred years simply because we are still so far from any really adequate knowledge process in the study of the whole sociosphere. Our sampling system is imperfect to the point of being embarrassing; we have no centralized information collection and processing; we operate in bits and pieces, by lights and flashes, and there is up to now no steady process of cumulation, prediction, and feedback in the sociosphere as a whole. I have argued, for instance, that if we were going to take the social sciences seriously we should at least establish a world network of social data stations, analogous to weather stations. They would take constant measurements and readings of the social system around them by standardized and carefully sampled methods and feed this information into a central processing agency as weather stations collect information about the atmosphere and feed it to weather bureaus. As a matter of fact we have not even established a global system of information about the atmosphere as yet, so that the global information system about the socio-sphere is still presumably at least a generation away. Once this is established, however, I suspect that there will be a rapid cumulation of knowledge, a rapid revision of theoretical images, and a correspondingly profound change in the rate of change of the social system itself.

We cannot, of course, predict what these changes will be. One of the facts about the knowledge process which is too little recognized is that in the case of knowledge, and, one might even add, technology, prediction of the future is impossible. That is, if we knew what we were going to know next year we would know it now. Hence there must always be a certain element of surprise in the knowledge process; surprise is an essential element in information. It is only by unexpectedness that knowledge increases. This does not mean, of course, that we cannot speculate usefully about the possible or even probable lines of advance of knowledge and technology. By the very nature of the knowledge process, however, these speculations must be subject to a large margin of error. Even though, therefore, we may have a good deal of confidence that social-science knowledge will continue to increase as it has done in the past, or even that its rate of increase may accelerate, what this new knowledge will reveal and particularly what new directions of social organization will be stimulated by it are things that we cannot know at the present time.

Even though we cannot predict the growth of social-science knowledge in detail, we can say something about the form which this has taken in the past and which it is likely to take in the future. Every great advance in science seems to have been associated with a twofold movement, as suggested earlier. One is the development of a new theoretical insight or point of view, a restructuring of the image of the world, which creates, as it were, evolutionary potential for the increase of knowledge. The second condition is an improvement in instrumentation, that is, in the methods by which information coming from the outside world can be detected, sampled, and processed. Thus the Copernican revolution involved in the first place a shift from the man-centered view of the universe to what might be called the system-oriented image, even though Copernicus himself got many of the essential details quite wrong. For instance, he still thought that the planets moved in circles. The success of the Copernican revolution, however, depended to a very large extent on the invention of the telescope, which enormously improved the information collection from the astronomical universe and permitted much more exact comparison of predictions with fulfillments.

In the social sciences likewise, advance seems to

have depended in the past on a combination of new theoretical insights and points of view with new methods for the collection, sampling, and processing of data. It is certainly no accident that population theory and the census came along at about the same time, at the end of the eighteenth century. It is perhaps no accident that Adam Smith's theoretical vision of free trade and natural liberty went hand in hand with a substantial improvement in trade statistics, or that Malthus's great vision of an underemployment equilibrium had to wait a hundred years before it was revived by Keynes, for it took that long to produce national income statistics. It seems to be easier, incidentally, to find examples in which a theoretical insight failed to make an impact because of the absence of information collection and processing devices than it is to find the reverse. It is not unreasonable, therefore, to look to the greatest changes in the future to come from the social telescopes and microscopes, that is, the development of accurate and consistent methods of information collection and processing. It is because I feel that we are only at the beginning of these developments in social information collection and processing that I am optimistic about the future of the social sciences. What the social sciences are going to do to man and his society, however, is another question, which I will leave to another day.

2

✪✪✪✪ **Economics and the Economy**

The social sciences sometimes excuse themselves for their inadequacies by the plea of youth. In the case of economics this plea can hardly be sustained, for economics has good claims to be regarded as the second oldest of the sciences, younger than physics but older than chemistry. If we regard the date of founding of a science as the moment when it acquires a theoretical model sufficiently integrated and powerful so that inferences can be drawn from it which can be tested, then classical physics certainly dates from Newton and economics from Adam Smith, whose *Wealth of Nations* in 1776 set up an internally consistent framework of equilibrium theory, especially in regard to relative prices, which all subsequent work has modified only in detail rather than in essence. Furthermore, Adam Smith had a better theory of economic development than most economists have today. By contrast, chemistry was floundering in the phlogiston theory at that time and did not achieve a real theoretical integration until Dalton in the 1820s. Darwin in biology comes still a generation later, psychology and sociology later still; indeed it can be argued that the biological sciences have still not really reached their Newtonian synthesis.

In spite of the fact that its basic theoretical formulations came rather early, it is only in the last thirty or forty years that economics has developed anything like an adequate system for the collection and processing of information about the economy. At the time of Adam Smith very little systematic information was available, and under the circumstances it is all the more astonishing that his theoretical formulation was as profound and insightful as it was. Many of the theoretical discussions at the time of David Ricardo in the first quarter of the nineteenth century were vitiated by the absence of any adequate statistics, economic information, or indexing. Even such a simple device as the index number of prices did not come into general use until 1870, though time series of individual prices and wages had been collected for a long time. Statistics of national income and its distribution, however, were virtually unknown before the twentieth century. Thus Malthus was unable to confirm or to test the profound theoretical insights of his later work, *The Principles of Political Economy*, in which he largely anticipated the Keynesian system, and by virtue of sheer forensic ability Ricardo won the day. A hundred years later Keynes dramatically reversed the judgment of history. But even the success of the Keynesian theory depended to a considerable extent on the parallel developments in national income statistics, by which, for instance, the inner structure of a great depression in terms of the virtual disappearance of investment and the failure of consumption or government expenditures to rise in a compensating manner was clearly revealed.

Considering now in greater detail the impact of economics and especially of economists on the economy, one thinks of five names or groups of names as having had a major impact. I am excluding the mercantilists and the physiocrats, the first because they represented as it were the distillation of popular wisdom rather than any great new theoretical insights, with the possible exception of Thomas Mun; and the latter because they did not have very much impact on anybody except perhaps on Adam Smith. The first great name, therefore, is Adam Smith, and his impact on the development of free trade is well known.

The free-trade argument, which is actually very subtle in *The Wealth of Nations* itself, can only be appreciated in the presence of a level of analysis of the economic system which clearly goes beyond what might be called a "folk economics." There has to be a concept of the economic system as a whole, of the problem of allocation of resources, an understanding of the way in which the price system in fact serves to allocate resources, an understanding of the fact that trade is a positive-sum game, as we would call it nowadays, in which both parties benefit, and an understanding of the advantages of specialization in the division of labor. By contrast the arguments of vulgar protectionism are derived substantially from folk images of economic processes, images which overweight the advantages to the few, which are concentrated, and underweight the disadvantages to the many, which are diffuse. Protection furthermore appeals to that hatred of the foreigner which is an unfortunate characteristic of the mass of mankind, and there may even be subtle psychoanalytic reasons behind the feeling that export is good and import is bad.

Adam Smith's demolition of the mercantilists was almost too complete, for as Keynes pointed out in what was a return to a kind of neo-mercantilism, a favorable balance of payments by increasing the money supply might well increase employment and output if a society were operating at less than full capacity. This, however, is a still more subtle argument, one which neither

Adam Smith nor his opponents could possibly have used. It is an extraordinary tribute to the clarity and the forensic power of *The Wealth of Nations* that it did in fact have such an impact on the economic policies not only of Great Britain but also for a time of other countries. After 1860, it is true, rising nationalism and perhaps a not wholly unreasonable desire to use the tariff to foster growth industries led to a gradual retreat from the Smithian principles. Nevertheless, the strong pressure in the last twenty or thirty years towards the relaxation of trade barriers and even the relative economic success in development of countries like Malaya, which have taken advantage of successful trade opportunities and have not been afraid to specialize, indicates that Adam Smith is still a very live force in the world.

Furthermore, one can see the impact of Adam Smith on the economic ideology of the United States, especially in regard to internal economic policy, in such matters as the antitrust legislation, the regulation of monopoly, and a long prejudice against even such relatively mild interventions into the price system as the minimum wage. In the last thirty or forty years, it is true, we have largely lost our prejudices against intervening in the price system, though it is by no means certain that we have always intervened very successfully or intelligently. The voices of the so-called Chicago School of economists—notably Milton Friedman and George Stigler—with their frequently trenchant criticism of the kind of intervention which we have actually had is a tribute to the persisting vitality of Adam Smith's frame of thought.

In the generation after Adam Smith we find Ricardo and Malthus, each of whom exercised a substantial influence on the social system though in rather different ways. Malthus gave his name to a whole doctrine, Malthusianism, and as a result has perhaps received a good deal of unmerited abuse and even praise. His first *Essay on Population*, published in 1798, can certainly claim to be one of the most influential books of the last two hundred years, and it is even more relevant today than it was then. His great contribution is what might be called a "miserific vision" of long-run equilibrium in which the only really effective means of eventually bringing the growth of population to a halt is starvation and misery.

In this respect Malthus as a thinker was premature. He was successful in influencing the policies of his day largely for the wrong reasons, because his doctrine provided what looked like a good excuse for a highly restrictive and punitive poor law. With the wisdom of hindsight we can now see that for his own day Malthus was quite wrong. He wrote at the beginning of an enormous expansion of the food supply, both through the occupancy of virgin lands and through substantial increases in yield per acre through scientific technology. Consequently, even though there has been an enormous increase in population since Malthus's day, the food supply until very recently has increased roughly in proportion, and indeed in the developed part of the world in a greater proportion.

Nevertheless, Malthus was right in pointing out that the food supply eventually could never keep up with the exponential growth of population, and today the Malthusian devil looms larger than ever. Even the socialists, who have always hated Malthus—not perhaps altogether unreasonably, in the light of the use which was made of his theories to beat down social change—are now being forced to admit that rapid population growth can undermine economic development and that the problem of a long-run equilibrium of population must eventually be faced. And "eventually" now means fairly soon.

It can be argued, therefore, that the immediate results of Malthus were rather disastrous. The English Poor Law of 1834, for instance, which is largely attributed to his influence, in fact may just have made poor old people a little more miserable than they otherwise would have been and may have had very little influence even on the growth of the English population. If the "Speenhamland" system of outdoor relief had continued, the poor would have been happier and the rate of economic development would not have been much affected. It is in our own day, however, that Malthus has really come into his own, and recognition of the desperate necessity for means of population control, of which, incidentally, he would certainly not have approved, has become almost a commonplace.

If Malthus came too early, in a certain sense Ricardo came too late. He codified and clarified the insights of Adam Smith into a body of abstract doctrine, and it can be argued forcibly that the very success of this body of doctrine repressed the growth of knowledge in economics for almost a century and had substantially adverse effects on economic policy. Malthus again, with the genius he seemed to have for being premature, developed in his *Principles of Political Economy* in 1836 a remarkable body of insights into what we now think of as macroeconomics and anticipated the Keynesian revolution by a hundred years. Ricardo won his argument with him, however, and it was Ricardian thought that dominated the next century, with its orthodoxy of the gold standard, low government activity, balanced budgets, and a punitive poor law.

The fact that the nineteenth century in both Britain and America was as successful as it was certainly indicated that as a long-run formula for development the Ricardian model made some sort of sense and was certainly more successful than, shall we say, the profligate and insecure systems of Latin America. Nevertheless, many costs may have been unnecessarily high—the hungry forties, the depressed seventies and eighties, the excessive swing in the business cycle, and so on. Perhaps the very success of the Ricardian framework was its undoing. By the 1920s and still more the 1930s it had become very clear that this framework was inadequate to deal with the problems of the day. It may well be, therefore, as Keynes has suggested, that if Ricardo had written a generation earlier and Malthus had been more systematic and successful in debate the nineteenth century would have been just as successful in development and a good deal happier in terms of social costs. Like all the "ifs" of history, however, this is something we can never really know.

If economics is willing to claim Karl Marx, then from the point of view of the sheer magnitude of one man's influence on human history the impact of economics can well claim to be enormous. Probably no man in human history to date has had such an enormous impact on the world social system, for good or for ill. It is true that the impact of Marx depends not so much on the fact that he was an economist, for his contributions to economics are neither very good nor very original, but on the fact that he was a prophet and an ideologist whose vision of the world seemed to meet the needs of a great many in the succeeding century who were committed to social change. A good deal of the power of Marxian thought rises out of its synthetic and systematic nature, the fact that it represents what I would describe as a premature synthesis of the social sciences into a total vision of society. For minds which are intolerant of intellectual ambiguities, which want to know all the answers, a total system like Marxism is very attractive. Whatever the reasons for the impact, however, its magnitude can hardly be denied, for a third of the world's population now lives under regimes which owe their inspiration to Marx.

It is certainly beyond the scope of this essay to attempt to draw up a balance sheet on Marxism, and indeed it is still too early to do this. Both the costs and the benefits are very large, and under these circumstances it is hard to determine whether one exceeds the other. On the benefit side, Marxism has undoubtedly provided the excuse for the transformation of stagnant societies and for the spread of education, science, and technology into parts of the world where it had previously made little impact. It has produced a positive and reasonably high rate of economic development in virtually all the countries that it has touched. It has done this, however, at a very high social cost arising mainly out of the inadequacies of Marxism as a social theory. It represents, indeed, a highly special case which has relevance to some places and periods but not to all. The ideology of class war and revolution, furthermore, has been extremely costly in terms of human suffering, and even in terms of development, and countries which have achieved development without revolution, like Japan, have achieved the benefits with only a fraction of the costs. Both intellectually and aesthetically Marxism has also been costly in the sense that it has frozen the societies which it has dominated in a mid-nineteenth century complex of ideas and even tastes. What strikes one about the socialist countries today is their extraordinary Victorianism, and perhaps one of the costs of ideology is that it always imprints on the society it dominates the patterns of a dead past.

Oddly enough, it could easily be argued that the benefits of Marxism on the whole have been enjoyed mainly by the non-Marxist societies. The main significance of Marx was that he challenged the legitimacy of private property, the market as a social organizer, bourgeois ideals, and the bourgeois state. To any challenge to legitimacy there has to be a response, and the response to this challenge in the West has been quite profound. In Toynbeean terms, one could argue that Marxism provided almost an optimum degree of challenge to those societies which were already fairly well developed, whereas the challenge was simply too great for those societies of northeastern Eurasia which had not yet reached the point in development where the challenge could be met without catastrophe. Certainly the capitalist world today is far different from what it was in 1848, and some of the difference at any rate is a result of the response to the Marxist challenge, though how much is hard to evaluate.

The main reason why Marxism has not been successful in the West is that the dynamics of distribution followed an entirely different course from that which the Marxist theory predicted. Marx thought that the total amount of the product going to the worker would be fairly stable and that hence the increase in the product would all go to the capitalist. What has happened in fact is that a very large increase in the product in Western societies has been achieved while the proportional shares have been fairly stable; actually, the proportion going to labor has been increasing. Instead of surplus value concentrating in the hands of the capitalists, therefore, it has been widely distributed throughout the whole population without the abolition of private property and without the development of centrally planned economies. Indeed it is in the centrally planned economies that the exploitation of labor—in the supposed interest of posterity, it is true—has been most severe. The failure of the Marxist prediction in the West is clear; what is not clear is how much of this was due to the inherent dynamics of a market-oriented society and how much of it was due to specific reactions in terms of economic policy arising out of the Marxist criticism. One can certainly argue that the change in the status of the labor movement, the rise of social security, the development of the progressive income tax, and so on, were in part at any rate responses to the Marxist challenge which produced a lot of benefit at a pretty low social cost.

Perhaps the great tragedy of Marxism as an ideology is that it was formulated before the great developments in mathematical economics, econometrics, and economic information collection and processing which have characterized the last hundred years and which have particularly flowered in the last third of a century. It is hard to associate this change with any single person, though Keynes certainly represents its prophet and visionary, even though he was not a very good mathematician or statistician. The impact of this "sophisticating" of economics has been very large in the last twenty years and promises to be even larger in the future. This sophisticating process has exhibited many of the characteristics of what might be called the middle stage in the development of a science, such as, for instance, characterized astronomy from Copernicus to Newton. There are shifts in fundamental vision, and in this regard it is not wholly unfair to compare Keynes with Copernicus, for the Keynesian revolution, like the

Copernican revolution, represents a shift from a man-centered, behind-the-eyeball view of the universe to what might be called the system-oriented view.

There have also been a number of false starts and blind alleys. It is at least questionable, for instance, whether the mathematizations due to A. A. Cournot (1834), Léon Walras (1870), and V. Pareto (1896) have done much more than refine and make explicit the fundamental system which is implied in the classical economics of Adam Smith and Ricardo, even though that was not written in explicit mathematical language. Similarly, the empirical work of Wesley Mitchell in the 1920s on the business cycle seems to have been something of a blind alley, though one with a good many useful exits along the way.

The really powerful combination has been that of Keynesian theory with the collection and processing of national income statistics. National income statistics have done for Keynes what the telescope did for Copernicus. It has enabled us to watch the motions of the system and its component parts almost from month to month, certainly from quarter to quarter, and hence has given us a system of information feedback that we did not possess before. This combination of econometric models of the total economy with an information system which enables us to make reasonable estimates of the parameters has given us a sense of "steersmanship" of the economy which was quite foreign to the world before 1930. This is a change which has crept up on us rather slowly, so that we are apt to be unaware of its magnitude. There are many indications, however, that we have passed a subtle watershed and that we have achieved, as it were, revolutionary change without revolution, which is the most desirable way to do it.

If one is looking for a date of passing the watershed (though, as in Chicago, it is hard to tell where the watershed is), one might seize on 1946, with the passage of the Full Employment Act creating the Council of Economic Advisors and the Joint Economic Committee in Congress. This represented, as it were, the legitimation of economics as a profession and the establishment of economists as "lords spiritual" in the precincts of both the White House and Congress. The process has had its ups and downs. The success of the 1964 tax cut, however, with the relatively high rates of development of the 1960s, is perhaps the first conscious breakthrough in the United States of what might be called "national income economics." In Europe and in Japan the success of this kind of economics has been even greater, and in the last twenty years there have been rates of development which have been quite unprecedented.

The sense that the Second World War represented

something of a watershed is enhanced if we draw the comparison between the twenty years which followed the First World War, from 1919–1939, with the twenty years following the Second World War, which have just ended, 1945–1965. The first twenty years were a total failure; they saw the fiasco of reparations, the economic collapse of the Great Depression, and the rise of Hitler, and they ended in the Second World War. In the socialist world, the period was even more disastrous; the economic collapse in Russia in 1921 and the disaster of the First Collectivization represented enormous breakdowns of the social system. In the "Third World" hardly any progress was made towards the abolition of the colonial system, and the international economy stagnated or even declined. It is hard, indeed, to avoid awarding these years an "F—" from the point of view of human welfare and decency. By contrast, the years from 1945–65 at least seem to deserve a "C." We have not had any great depression; unemployment in the United States has rarely risen above 6 per cent of the labor force; reasonable rates of economic growth have been maintained; and in Europe and Japan and even some other countries, extraordinary rates of growth have been achieved, as much as 8 per cent per annum per capita in Japan, over 7 per cent in West Germany, and 5 or 6 per cent in a good many other countries. The colonial system has largely been disbanded, and even though the cold war and the world war industry represent an enormous burden on mankind of about $120 billion a year, at least there has been some progress towards international organization and peaceful coexistence, and we are certainly further from the Third World War in 1966 than we were from the Second World War in 1940, when it was actually under way.

One certainly would not wish to credit economics with all these achievements. Even if we only credit it with 10 per cent of the difference, however, this is very sizable. If, for instance, we had had a great depression in the United States in the 1950s instead of a mild stagnation, it would unquestionably have cost us $500 billion and an enormous worsening of the international climate. We certainly do not put much more than $100 million a year into economics, so that the rate of return on this investment could easily be of the order of thousands of a per cent per annum. It is not surprising, therefore, that the economics profession finds itself today in a rather self-congratulatory mood. Professor Schumpeter once said to me, "How nice economics was before anybody knew anything!" meaning, of course, that in the days before national income statistics, economists could spin any theories they wanted to and nobody could check up on them. Today the feedback from reality is great enough that it may

cramp the artistic style of the theorist, but it unquestionably increases the power of the discipline.

The impact of economics is by no means confined
to stabilization policy and the cure of unemployment.
In the last twenty years we have seen the development
of something called variously "management science,"
"'operations research," and "decision theory." This is
a body of theory, information collection, processing,
and pratice which in a sense emerged out of economics
but which has now established itself as a fairly inde-
pendent discipline, still, of course, within the social
sciences.

Decision theory is a set of mathematical variations
on the theme that everybody does what he thinks is
best at the time, and management science consists
essentially of a variety of techniques for defining and
identifying the "best" out of a set of possible choices.
The first step is to define the field of choice itself,
which might be called the "agenda"; the second step is
to define a function which enables us to order the
elements of the field of choice and then select the one
which stands at the top of the list. When the number
of elements in the field of choice is small and valuation
procedures are simple, folk knowledge is quite adequate to deal with the problem. When, however, the
number of elements in the field of choice becomes
very large, sophisticated procedures have to be devised

if rational choices are to be made. Development in the fields of applied mathematics such as linear or non-linear programming consists essentially in devices for ordering large fields of choice through orderly mathematical procedures. The practitioners of management science now number several thousand, and they have unquestionably made a substantial contribution to the development of more realistic and sophisticated decisions in organizations of all kinds, both public and private.

At the moment it is virtually impossible to evaluate the impact of this movement, for it has not really been in existence a long enough time. As with everything else, one has to balance the gains against possible losses. The gains represent decisions made with the aid of these sophisticated procedures which are more profitable to the decision-maker or perhaps to the society at large than those which would be made without them. The gain here is the difference between our evaluation of those elements of the set of choices which would be selected in the presence of sophisticated procedures and those elements which would be selected without them. Here a great deal depends on the nature of the utility function, as it is called, that is, the evaluations of the various elements in the set of choice. If there are only a few elements in the set which are very highly valued, with all the other elements having a very low valuation, mistakes in decision can be very important. If on the other hand there are a large number of elements as it were bracketed at the top of the list, and all of about equal value, then a decision is unimportant; anything we decide will be all right. Unfortunately, we do not know enough about the value functions of our society to know how far one or the other of these patterns prevails. If it is the second, then refined decision-making processes do not add much to our total welfare; if the first condition prevails, they may add a great deal.

There are also possibilities of certain costs of sophisticated decision-making procedures. They may, for instance, give an illusion of certainty to the decision-maker in situations which have objective uncertainty, and uncertain situations require a very different kind of behavior and different decision procedures from certain ones. In an uncertain situation, for instance, he who hesitates is frequently saved; and an important aspect of decision-making consists of the capacity not to pre-empt the future but to leave decisions open. Sophisticated decision procedures may lead to premature closure, to too little emphasis on liquidity and hesitation, and hence perhaps to disastrous mistakes. One worries about this especially in the international system, where pseudosophistication could easily lead to greater instability. The only remedy for that little learning which is a dangerous thing is, however, more of the same, or perhaps more of a different kind of learning. There is never any way back to ignorance, even when ignorance is bliss. Consequently we may expect that the decision-making process will become more and more sophisticated and that as a result fewer mistakes in decision will be made.

The long-run consequences of a substantial improvement in decision-making processes may be rather unexpected. There might, for instance, be some sacrifice of long-run development for short-run stability. The capacity to make mistakes and suffer the consequences is certainly an important aspect of the evolutionary process, and sophisticated decision procedures may easily introduce a diminution in the rate both of social mutation and selection. Improved decision procedures, for instance, could result in increasing the duration of life of organizations of all kinds. What this would do to the long-run rate of social evolution is not clear, but this perhaps is something that we can leave the future to worry about.

It is clear that economics as a social science has now reached a degree of sophistication where its impact on the economy is very substantial and is likely to be even greater in the future. It can hardly be denied as far as economics is concerned that we now know something and that this knowledge can be applied. Knowing something, however, is not knowing everything, and we still have a long way to go. I would not like to give the impression that economics has reached its summit of achievement and that there are no more problems to be solved. In fact there is a great deal yet to be done, both in theory and in the development of information collection and processing, and the mood of the economist should not be that of resting on his oars and enjoying his laurels but rather pulling up his sleeves and getting about a number of very urgent jobs.

One of the biggest unsolved problems, in economic policy certainly, is that of the intelligent use of the price system. This problem has two aspects. One is the problem of the general level of prices and money wages. The other is the problem of the relative price structure. Even the problem of the general level is still quite unsolved, and it remains the Achilles' heel of national income economics. It is fairly easy to stabilize or do anything we want with the national income in dollar terms. If we want this, for instance, to grow at 5 per cent per annum, suitable adjustments of the fiscal and monetary system would easily permit this, and we are certainly within sight of devising a social-cybernetic apparatus which would keep the rate of growth of the gross national product in dollar terms within easily tolerable limits.

The dollar value of the national product, however, is a product of two aggregates or indices, and is equal to the quantity of output in real terms multiplied by the money price level of this output. Within a stable or controlled total dollar value of the national output, it would be quite possible to have substantial fluctuations in opposite directions of the quantity level and the price level. What we really want to control, however, is the quantity level. It is the fluctuations in this or the failure of this to grow which causes trouble, and the ideal of aggregative economic policy would be a steady growth of the total quantity of output at some reasonable figure. The dollar value we know how to control fairly well; the price level we do not know how to control. The great dilemma of stabilization policy is that before we reach the ideal output or full employment, the market forces of the economy seem to create an unacceptable rate of increase in the level of prices and money wages.

Up to now the only institutional device we have discovered to deal with this is Presidential anger, institutionalized in the form of guidelines, and this is a system that would not stand very much strain. It may be, as Gardner Means has suggested, that we shall find a solution to this problem through certain modifications of the tax system which will discriminate against increases in income due to increased prices or money wages, but this still seems to be fairly far in the future.

When we come to the problem of the ideal structure of relative prices, the situation both in theory and in practice can only be described as deplorable. In the United States, for instance, we are only just beginning to realize that a great deal of our intervention in the relative price structure, which was motivated at least in part by a desire to redistribute income towards the poor, has in fact redistributed income towards the rich. This is certainly true of agricultural policy, for instance, where trying to solve the problem of agricultural poverty by raising the relative prices of agricultural commodities has resulted in subsidizing the rich farmers, who after all have a lot to sell, and doing very little for the poor farmers except chasing them out of agriculture altogether—which, as a matter of fact, may not be a bad solution. In terms of economic development and rate of technological change, agricultural policy has in fact been an uproarious success, but in terms of the objectives of social justice which originally gave rise to it, it is open to very severe criticism.

One could give a great many examples of cases in which governmental distortion of the price system has had a very dubious result. Even in the case of public education, where we have supposedly subsidized education by making it either cheap or free, a considerable amount of the subsidy has gone to the rich or middle classes. The local tax system which supports these educational subsidies is frequently extremely regressive, so that actually it taxes the poor to educate the middle classes and the rich. It is not surprising under the circumstances that human resources are wasted and that we have a problem of self-perpetuating pockets of poverty which the system of public education completely fails to touch. If we were willing to use the price system more, to charge full-cost fees and to use public funds to provide scholarships, many of the present economic problems of the educational system might be solved. The state universities are an even more flagrant case of subsidizing the rich by a regressive tax system in the interest of what is supposed to be equal opportunity, which in fact is nothing of the sort. Even social security is open to charges that it is a much heavier burden on the poor than on the rich and that it actually represents very little in the way of redistribution. It also involves a substantial tax on the present generation of young people, who in effect are buying insurance and annuities at very poor rates in order to subsidize their improvident grandparents.

When we look at things like antitrust policy, the confusion about what we ought to do about the relative price structure becomes all the more patent. While the antitrust legislation in the United States can be

defended on the grounds that it has created a mild ir-
ritant for decision-makers of the business community
which has prevented them taking certain easy ways
out and hence has pushed them in the direction of
fostering technological improvement, it cannot be
defended on the grounds of any logical consistency
or on the grounds of any theory about ideal prices or
even ideal forms of economic organization. When we
turn to the regulated industries, we see a considerable
success with the American Telephone and Telegraph
Company and a disastrous failure with the railroads,
so here again it is clear that the solutions of the past
do not necessarily apply to the present.

At the root of a great deal of the failure of what we
might call microeconomic policy lies a serious defect
in economic theory itself—its inability to deal with the
larger problems of the distribution of income. There
are still many unsolved problems, for instance, even in
the question of the incidence of taxation on the distribution of income. We still do not really know the
extent to which manipulation of the price system, for
instance through minimum wages or subsidies, affects
the overall distribution. We also do not have any
adequate theory of the long-run distribution of property, on which the distribution of income in part rests.
These are technical problems which we cannot go into
now, but they deserve to be noted in case economists

get a little intoxicated with their present success.

Another problem of enormous importance where the contribution of economics is at the least ambiguous is that of economic development. The demand for rapid economic development on the part of the poor countries is now so insistent that the economics of development has become extremely fashionable and has a large market. Nevertheless, the economic models of development leave much to be desired and have by no means always been helpful. Partly this is because the developmental process goes far beyond economics in the narrow sense and involves a unified social dynamics which still exists only in embryo. Hence it is perhaps unfair to blame economics for what is really a failure of general social science. Economists, however, are not altogether guiltless of presuming to know more than they do and of giving advice when they should have been doing research. It is clear that economic development involves profound cultural change as well as economic change in the narrow sense, and though we do have the beginnings of a general developmental theory, for instance in the works of Everett E. Hagan and David C. McClelland, we may need to wait another twenty years before we see in terms of success and failure how some of these principles work out.

In conclusion, one may note that the problem of

what might be called comparative economic systems still remains to be solved in a scientific, as opposed to an ideological, manner. The cold war, even ideologically, has certainly diminished in intensity in the last ten years, and economics can take some credit for this. The careful analytical study of socialist economies on the part of Western economists and of capitalist economies on the part of socialist economists have produced, if not agreement, at least a substantial area of professional discourse and mutual understanding. It can be recognized, of course, that the choice between a centrally planned economy and a market-based economy depends on non-economic factors more than it does on strictly economic ones. Nevertheless, a good deal remains to be done in what might be called the cost-benefit analysis of economic institutions, especially now that substantial modifications in both socialist and capitalist institutions have proceeded to the point where different countries provide a very wide spectrum of overall economic institutions. I would hesitate to suggest at this stage that we could do a cost-benefit analysis, shall we say, of the American financial system and compare this with Yugoslav investment planning; but at least some more or less rational comparisons might be in order. The conclusion of such a study might well be that the differences between the various systems are not significant enough to warrant putting much effort into changing them except by a succession of incremental changes, which would make the outlook look rather bad for revolution. However, it should also be possible to do a cost-benefit analysis on revolution, at least in a rough way, which might easily produce rather radical changes in the popularity of various ideologies. All this, of course, is very speculative. It suggests, however, that there is a large field of research here for the future, which might have a substantial effect in reconciling the present world split.

The general conclusion of this chapter, then, would seem to be that, as far as economics is concerned, we look to the past with modest satisfaction and to the future with hope. I trust that it is not merely the fact that I am a professional economist which gives rise to the optimism of this conclusion, but at least in a day of constant bemoaning it is nice to be able to take at least a modest satisfaction in something. In the next chapter, I fear, not even that small pleasure will be granted.

3

The Impact of the Social Sciences on the International System

I have selected the international system quite deliberately as that part of the sociosphere on which the social sciences have probably made the least impact and which is still being operated largely by folk knowledge or at best literary knowledge. It is a part of the social system, furthermore, where the difficulties of applications of social-science methodology are considerable, but where, nevertheless, the payoffs seem to be enormous, and where, therefore, we may reasonably expect to find a good deal of energy applied in the next generation.

To illustrate the present condition of the international studies, I can quote a story told to me by a distinguished colleague who was a member of a committee to investigate the problems of research into the international system. One member of the committee was a distinguished gentleman from the State Department who said he didn't really think that research into the international system was necessary; that whenever a problem came to his desk he always consulted Thucydides, who usually had the answer. The chilling thought occurred to me in this story that what we are fighting in Vietnam is the Peloponnesian War; but it illustrates at any rate the rather sharp contrast between what might be called a literary approach to the international system and the social-scientific approach.

We should begin, perhaps, by attempting to define the international system, at least roughly. The principal elements of the international system consist of sovereign governments, sovereign particularly in their relations with each other. These, however, do not exhaust the field; there are also dependent territories, international organizations such as the United Nations and its various agencies, and even private organizations which operate across national boundaries such as international businesses and the so-called NGOs (non-governmental organizations) like the Red Cross, international scientific associations, and so on.

In the case of the sovereign national state, a rough distinction can be made between that part of its activity which is devoted to the international system and that part which deals with domestic affairs. The "foreign affairs" which constitute the international-system element consist of its state department or foreign office, its armed forces, its espionage services, perhaps some aspects of its international trade organizations, especially if it is a socialist state—all those parts of its organization, in fact, which are mainly concerned with external relations.

The distinction between domestic and foreign affairs, however, is not a clear one and has become increasingly clouded in recent years. Many aspects of the organization and behavior of a national state which are thought of as concerned primarily with domestic matters in fact have a profound influence on the international system. A good example of this is American agricultural policy, which one would ordinarily categorize in the purely domestic section of government activity but which, because of its effect in generating agricultural surpluses and the attempt to solve this problem by shipping the surpluses abroad, has in fact become a major element of the international system. Similarly, if a state has a revolutionary ideology and seeks to propagate this, or even if it is permeated by a religion which indulges in missionary enterprise, its domestic character will have profound effects on the international scene. Even though the

distinction between domestic and foreign affairs, therefore, should not be discarded altogether, it should be
recognized that the national "actor," as it is sometimes
called in the international system, is a complex and
interrelated subsystem of the sociosphere and that all
aspects of its condition and movement may affect the
international system in greater or less degree.

It must be recognized also that the dynamics of the
international system is affected not merely by the conscious behavior or policy of states but is profoundly
affected by those latent processes, which may not be
the result of any conscious decisions, by which different societies rise and fall in relative population, income, and power. One of the most important elements
of the international system, in fact, is the relative rate
of economic development of different countries; for
power in the international system is a function in large
part of the gross national product, and as relative
changes occur in this, with one nation growing faster
than another until it overtakes its former superior,
there may be shifts in the international "pecking order"
which may be difficult to achieve without serious conflict or even war. We always have to look at the international system, therefore, as a subsystem within the
sociosphere with strong interactions with the econosphere, with the development of science and technology, with ideological movements, and so on, which are

ordinarily regarded as outside the international system.

All social systems are organized by three types of activity—threats, exchange, and integrative activity; and the international system is no exception. Unlike the economic system, however, which tends to be dominated by exchange, the international system is dominated by threats, at least in terms of resources employed. The war industry, that is that part of activity devoted to the armed forces and their supply, and which may be defined as that part of the total product of society which is paid for by the military budget, is by far the largest part of the international system in terms of sheer dollars. The world war industry amounts to over $120 billion a year, perhaps $150 billion. It is primarily designed to preserve the credibility of threats and counterthreats, usually tacit or implicit, although occasionally specific; and it represents an activity perhaps ten or twenty times as large as the activity devoted to diplomacy and other aspects of the international system.

Exchange, however, is not an unimportant element in the system and characterizes not only the negotiation of such things as trade agreements, which impinge directly on the economic system, but also the negotiation of treaties, alliances, recognition, and so on, which involve diplomatic bargaining. It is at least roughly true to suggest that whereas the armed forces represent the embodiment of the threat system, diplomacy in international relations involves mainly the conduct of exchange.

Underlying both the threat system and the exchange system in international relations is the integrative system. This consists of activity directed to establishing and maintaining such things as protocol, ceremony, dynastic marriages (in the old days at least), cultural exchange, and propaganda, and other activity directed towards the establishment of legitimacy, status, respect, affection, and other relationships of the integrative system.

A good deal of integrative activity on the part of the national state is also directed towards its own people, who have to be taught to regard the threat system as legitimate and who have to be taught to love their country and to make sacrifices for it, to exhibit attitudes of loyalty, and so on. The public education system is often a most important element in this integrative activity directed towards a country's own citizens. Even religion, insofar as it is a national religion and a symbol of the unity of the nation, plays an important part in developing attitudes of love and loyalty towards the nation. The family also is a very important transmitter of integrative relationships. Children are taught in the family to identify with the parents, and this means of course identifying with everything that the parents identify themselves with.

Nothing perhaps illustrates more clearly the difference between the literary approach to knowledge about social systems and the social-scientific approach than the attitude towards the integrative system. On the whole, the literary approach takes this for granted, and the question, "Why do people love their country?" would never really occur to the non-scientist. Science, however, because its point of view attempts at least to transcend the cultural peculiarities of the scientist, is entitled to ask questions of this kind and indeed finds them most interesting.

The cost of the present international system is very high. The world war industry, as we have seen, costs something between $120 billion and $150 billion. If we add to this the cost of the diplomatic establishment, this will probably add another $5 billion to $10 billion; and if we add as we should an estimate of the discounted probability of destruction in future wars, on fairly reasonable assumptions we could easily add another $100 billion or $200 billion. Even the world war industry itself is roughly equivalent to the total income of the poorest half of the world's population, even though it is not more than 10 per cent of the gross world product. By comparison, the resources which are put into the world integrative system are almost trivial. The total budget of all the international organizations, for instance, including the United Nations, special funds, UNESCO, the International Labor Organization, and all the other international agencies only amounts to about a third of a billion dollars, or about 0.3 per cent of the world war industry. Even the amount spent on cultural exchange, international education, and so on, likewise is relatively insignificant, so that it is not unreasonable to state that the threat system completely dominates the international system at present. As the threat system is apt to be a negative-sum game its overall productivity is very low, and it is not surprising that throughout history there have been strong attempts to contain it and modify it.

In considering the overall dynamics of the international system, as we have partly noted already, an important distinction can be made between the latent processes which are not the result of any conscious decisions and the manifest processes, as Robert Merton calls them, which are the result of conscious decisions. The latent processes include not only the broad economic processes of development or decline but also certain political processes such as the development of internal factions and splits, the rise or decline of the internal power of monarchs, military forces, a capitalist elite, a communist elite, a church, a reformation or a revolution, and so on, a great deal of which takes place outside the will of any decision-maker. Even war, as Tolstoy brings out so brilliantly in *War and Peace*, becomes a great impersonal process largely out of the control of particular heads of state, generals, or decision-makers. These latent processes also include what must be regarded as random elements, that is, elements of the system which cannot be predicted from previous information. Events such as the assassination of President Kennedy and the birth and rise of a charismatic political leader like Hitler or Nkrumah must be regarded as random from the point of view of the system itself. It is this mixture of ordered or deterministic latent processes with strong random elements which makes the epistemological problem in social systems generally and the international system in particular so very difficult. We constantly tend to interpret random phenomena as if they were in fact conforming to deterministic patterns; this, indeed, is what we really mean by superstition. On the other side we also fail to detect what are the real patterns in the non-random elements of the system.

The manifest aspects of the international system consist of decisions, taken consciously by the principal decision-makers of the system. These decision-makers in some cases may be the heads of state, prime ministers, dictators, cabinets, secretaries of state, and so on, though sometimes important decisions are made lower down in the hierarchy to which the top decision-makers have to conform, whether they wish to or not. The top decision-makers can easily be caught in a trap of their own commitments and information systems, and hence they may have much less freedom of action than might appear at first sight. The sort of decisions which are made are, for instance, decisions to raise or to lower the level of armaments, to make specific threats, to advance or withhold recognition, to mobilize troops, to make conciliatory gestures, to declare war or to sue for peace, and so on. All these decisions are made in the light of some kind of image of the world and particularly some kind of image of the international system. The decision-maker will have an image of his own nation and his responsibilities towards it and also an image of other nations with which he has relations. These various images have no obligation to be consistent, and many of the difficulties of the international system arise from this fact.

Up to now it is fair to say that the images of the international system on which the decisions of its decision-makers are based are derived mainly from a mixture of folk and literary knowledge processes. They do not usually involve the careful sampling, the theoretical models checked by constant feedback and testing, which are characteristic of the scientific process. The international system indeed is characterized by an

information system which is almost designed to produce false images, at least in the short run, and it is
not surprising, therefore, that it is so costly or that
the decisions made are often so disastrous. Its information system consists in the first place of bureaucratic
organizations—state departments, foreign offices, departments of external affairs, whatever they may be
called—which tend to be operated by a gentlemanly,
aristocratic, and literary elite whose members are un-
familiar and indeed hostile towards the scientific processes and indeed belong almost exclusively to that one
of C. P. Snow's "two cultures" which is least friendly
towards an understanding of scientific method.

The information which is processed in this bureauc-
racy is collected in the first instance by diplomats
and spies and, insofar as it is public information, the
public press. Both diplomats and spies are notoriously
unreliable because of the nature of the sample of the
information which their respective subcultures produce. Diplomats live in a world of their own, principally composed of other diplomats, and are largely
insulated from the ordinary life of the country to which
they are accredited. Even though they have specialized staffs which collect information it is very rare
that embassies will be staffed by social scientists.

The subculture of spying organizations, because of
its extraordinarily intense emotive content and strong

value system, is apt to produce even more unreliable information. The whole information, collection, and processing system in the international system, as a matter of fact, is apt to be perverted by the strong emotive affects which characterize it. The national state in these days at any rate is a quasi-religious organization, attracting very strong loyalties or even disloyalties, and hence its whole information system has a built-in filter that tends to remove what is disagreeable or non-conforming to existing images.

Moreover, any hierarchy has a problem in that the success of an individual within it depends on his capacity to please his superiors, and he frequently tends to please his superiors by passing on to them that information which he thinks will please them. When information goes through a number of layers of a hierarchy it is apt to be quite distorted by the time it gets to the top. Hence the top decision-makers are apt to be insulated from the real world and receive only that information which confirms their previously established images.

It is no wonder that under these circumstances the international system operates so badly, that it is so costly, and that it provides so little of the security that is supposed to be its principal benefit. It is precisely the defects in its information system which make the probability of war so high and the cost of war so great. War indeed can be regarded as the ultimate process of reality-testing of the threat system, but it is a process of reality-testing that reminds one of the man who jumped off the Empire State Building in order to test the law of gravity. One of the great problems in the international system is how to develop a learning process in which we do not have to fall over the cliffs in order to learn where they are.

It is my contention that the social-scientific process of collecting and processing information and of modifying images of the system can be applied to the international system in a much greater degree than is now being done. It must be admitted, however, that the international system presents peculiar problems which make it more difficult as an object of scientific study than, shall we say, the economic system. The relative success of social-scientific method in economics and its relative lack of success in the international system is not so much a reflection of the body of skill of the various practitioners, though this may have something to do with it. Rather does it reflect the intrinsic difficulty of the international system itself.

The economist studies the interaction of a very large number of decisions. The random element in the system is thereby diminished, and the role of the personal decision-maker is not so important. This is particularly true of aggregative economics; it is even true of economics at the level of supply-and-demand analysis. Economics also has a great advantage in possessing what A. C. Pigou called "the measuring rod of money."

In the international system, by contrast, the key decision-makers are few in number and their inter-actions are accordingly complex. The international system is much more like a duopoly or oligopoly in economics, where we have the interaction of a few sellers. In this case the personalities of the decision-makers may be important. We cannot assume that individual differences cancel out in the mass, and even though in organizations the behavior of a role occupant such as a president or prime minister is determined in considerable measure by the role which he occupies and the information system which surrounds him, dif-ferent decision-makers in the same role will make different decisions and it cannot be assumed that the structure of the organization determines the decisions which are made in it. Under these circumstances there are genuinely random elements in the system which are not susceptible to scientific analysis, though scien-tific analysis may be helpful in protecting us from drawing false conclusions and inferring false system-atizations from what are essentially random events.

Furthermore, in the international system, values, even peculiar values, are of great importance in determining the nature of decisions. We cannot assume, for instance, as we do as a first approximation in economics, a simple value system like profit maximization. Attempts have been made to find a substitute for profit in the notion of the national interest, but the national interest is a highly subjective and evanescent variable which depends to a considerable extent on what the particular rulers of a country are interested in. The national interest of Spain may be the promotion of Catholicism and of Russia the promotion of communism, or it may in the case of the smaller states be the promotion of the bank balance of the ruler in a Swiss bank. Some nations are interested in expanding their power and territory, some are not; and in view of this wide variety of interests the concept of national interest would seem almost to disintegrate.

In any adequate theory of the international system, therefore, the process of the learning of values must be included. We cannot take values for granted, as we largely do in economics, assuming that people always prefer to be richer than poorer. There are exceptions to this even in economics, but in the international system there are so many exceptions that it is hard to find any rule at all. These international value systems, furthermore, are held with strong emotive affect, which in turn, as we have noted earlier, tends to pervert the information system, and hence the image of the world is itself a product of the value system. If there is one norm in international decision-making, it seems to be wishful thinking.

A further difficulty arises because one of the major characteristics of the international system is secrecy, and secrecy is the greatest enemy of science of all kinds. The international system has a mystique of its own, as reflected in its most absurd, perhaps, in the James Bond pattern, where secrecy, drama, sadism and hostility are essential items. Under these circumstances, what I have elsewhere called the "heroic" ethic rather than the economic ethic tends to take over, and decisions are made not on the basis of careful weighing of gain against loss but on the basis of heroic attitudes, death wishes, and the whole panoply of political paranoia. In the heroic ethic, indeed, a positive value is attached to having no choice—here I stand and I can do no other—theirs not to reason why, theirs but to do and die—and so on; and hence there is frequently an almost conscious narrowing of alternatives to one which is clearly bad but also unique.

In spite of all these difficulties, I still argue that the social-scientific revolution in the international system is not only possible but has actually begun. As we saw earlier, the advance of scientific knowledge in any system tends to depend on two parallel developments. One is the development of new theoretical insights which are able to identify the essential variables of the system and relate them in a logically consistent way in a theoretical model, which is then capable of continual modification under a process of prediction and testing and continuing experience. The work of a considerable group of theorists of the international system in the last ten years has brought us very close to this, although in the absence of an adequate information system it is hard to be sure that the theory is really testable.

The pioneer of this theoretical movement was Lewis Richardson, whose theories of arms races, war moods, and statistics of deadly quarrels constitute a remarkable body of pioneering work. Like all pioneering work performed in the absence of colleagues or of an intellectual community of scholars working in the same field, Richardson's work is uneven. Brilliant insights are apt to be followed by quite simple fallacies. Nevertheless it is a work of great importance, and the present generation of international systems theorists look back to him, and also to that other and more "respectable" pioneer, Quincy Wright, long associated with the University of Chicago, as the founding fathers of the field. Game theory has provided a certain body of mathematical devices which have been useful, though its usefulness is somewhat limited; and in the work of men like Thomas Schelling, Karl Deutsch,

David Singer, Charles McClelland, Robert North, Morton Kaplan, and others among whom I might include myself, we do seem to be within sight at least of a general theory of the international system which could be subject to study and modification in the direction of reality through a process of careful observation and testing. We might call this "international-systems theory" to differentiate it from the literary and speculative theories which have characterized political thought from the time of Aristotle, which often have a great deal of value and provide, indeed, profound insights, but which do not constitute an organic, continuously growing and developing model such as characterizes genuinely scientific images.

International-systems theory, then, may be said to have the following characteristics:

1) It is Copernican in the sense that the system is looked at as a whole and not from the perspective of any particular nation. This is what might be called a systems approach rather than a foreign-policy approach. It does not take the environment of any nation as a given factor, but regards all nations as constituting the environment of the others. This does for the international system what, shall we say, Laplace did for astronomy or Walras for economics. It cannot be expressed in any simple system of equations and probably should not be, though the general model of the

war industry, in which the military budget of each nation is written as a function of the military budget of all others, is of enormous interest and throws a good deal of light on the realities of the system. Any such explicit model, however, must be recognized as highly abstract, but the general principle remains in the concrete, that the behavior of each depends on the behavior of all.

2) It is a parametric theory in the sense that it implies the mutual interaction of a great many variables and hence gets beyond the notions of simple cause and effect which are so popular with the historians. The simplest parametric models are those of static or stationary equilibrium, which perhaps are not very realistic in the international system. Nevertheless, equilibrium models should not be despised, for there are periods in the system of what might be called quasi-stability, and the notion of a dynamic system as a succession of equilibrium states is always very useful.

3) It is a dynamic theory in the sense that it recognizes the dynamic processes of interaction, for instance in arms races, the crucial significance of learning processes, and the long, latent processes of population growth, economic growth, political maturation, and so on. A theory of the international system can never rest content with equilibrium models, for dynamic change is of the essence of the international system, and equi-

librium models can only be looked upon as a stepping-stone to a genuine dynamic theory.

4) It is an institutional theory in that it recognizes the importance of institutions, of organizational structures, of channels of communication, of constitutions and legal systems, of various procedures by which roles are filled, and so on. In the international system, as we have seen, we cannot depend on any simple behavioral principles, such as maximizing behavior, which serve us in economics. International behavior must be studied in a context of close observation of reality. Allowance has to be made for apparently irrational elements. The symbolic elements in the system must be stressed; there are, for instance, certain salient events which have an impact on the images of the international system far beyond their apparently intrinsic importance, and there must, therefore, be room in the system for a wide variety of behavioral principles. Insofar as behavior is conditioned by organizational structure, cultural habits, and constitutional forms, these also must be considered explicitly.

5) It is a transactional theory in the sense that it lays stress not only on the characteristics of the actors themselves but on the relations and transactions among them. This is sometimes carried to the point where the actors themselves almost seem to disappear or are broken down into a succession of related trans-

actions, and this perhaps is going too far. Nevertheless, in a theory of this kind stress must be laid on the fact that the principal significance of the descriptive state of the actor lies in the impact of that state on the transactions with which he may engage and that these transactions in their turn create the states of the future.

6) It is an aggregative theory in the sense that it looks for methods of reducing and indexing very large bodies of information into simple quantitative indices which indicate the essential characteristics of the system. In this sense it seeks to devise an information-processing apparatus which will separate the merely accidental and random elements of the system from the regular and persistent patterns. This of course is not to deny significance to random events, which in a system of this kind, as we have already seen, can be of great importance. It seeks rather an image of the world which can recognize random events and not be unduly influenced by them and which can learn to take them for what they are. At this point stochastic or probabilistic models may be extremely useful in describing the essentially systematic characteristics of the processess. The theory here has to get away from mere narrative and succession—A did x, so B did y—and perceive the larger and more stable patterns

of the system. The epistemological problems here are severe but, one hopes, not insuperable.

It would take a large volume even to outline the actual content of the theory the properties of which are suggested above, and no attempt will be made to do this here. What must be stressed, however, is that the theory will be largely impotent and incapable of modification under testing unless the international system's apparatus for collecting and processing information is enormously improved. In spite of the difficulties which were mentioned earlier, it certainly seems possible to achieve a major improvement in the accuracy and the significance of the information collected from the international system. The key to this process is collecting information for its own sake. We notice this, for instance, even in economics, that as long as the information system of the economy consisted of information collected as a by-product of other activities, for instance the taxation or the collection of customs duties, we got no clear view of the system as a whole. It was not until we began to collect information directly for its own sake, in censuses and sample surveys, that we began to get a picture of the total economy which was reasonably well sampled and undistorted. Similarly in the international system, its existing information collection and processing is enormously biased by other purposes, either the justification of existing national attitudes or the operation of national threat systems, or even the interests of the readers of newspapers. It would now be possible, however, to set up a system of information collection and processing which should be scientific in the sense that the information is collected for its own sake, not for other purposes, and that it should be collected by processes of careful sampling and statistically ritualistic procedures which permit comparability of concepts and the aggregation of information collected. What we need, in fact, is a world network of social data stations, something like weather stations, perhaps one to each five million people. These should for the most part be associated with universities, where they could perform the function of a laboratory for training and research, as do meteorological stations. We cannot expect to know very much about the atmosphere unless we have a world network of weather stations, and similarly we cannot expect to know much about the sociosphere until we have a world network of social data stations. With such a network and a centralized information processing center, not only could we obtain accurate demographic and economic data but we could also obtain indices of hostility, perceptions of threat, changes in value systems, and so on, which are now largely inaccessible. Surveillance from satellites is a very poor substitute for listening to what people actually say, for it is the communications of people that constitute by far the larger part of the social system.

There would, of course, be political problems in the collection and publishing of data of this kind. A system of social data stations would be something of a threat to the secrecy and the mystique, what one is almost tempted to call the masculine mystique, of the international system; and insofar as political power rests upon secrecy and ignorance, the development of a social-scientific apparatus for the increase of knowledge would be regarded as a threat. One can only hope that the payoffs of such a system in the improvement of international decision-making and the lowering of the cost of the international system would be so enormous and so obvious that this would gradually overcome the political resistances. A good deal of hostility towards the social sciences, however, is going to have to be overcome, especially in the light of the fact that the culture of the international system on the whole is hostile to science, which it regards, perhaps quite rightly, as a threat to its traditional values.

I am not suggesting, of course, that an international-system science of this kind would solve all the problems of the international system or even guarantee a stable peace. Stable peace has been developed in parts of the international system, such as North America and Scandinavia, even within the present international information system, through a process of what might almost be described as accidental folk learning. Under some circumstances, moreover, increased knowledge of the system could easily increase tensions and in the beginning is quite likely to do so as the traditional power structures are threatened by the new knowledge. We should never claim that scientific knowledge is a perfect substitute for folk and literary knowledge, for it is not. Especially in the light of the enormous complexity of the social system, there will probably always be a place for the folk knowledge of the politician and the literary knowledge of the bureaucrat. There is good reason to suppose, however, that the development of an international-system science would enormously diminish the costs of the international system and increase its benefits. An international system is quite conceivable in which the costs of security are down to those of internal police, yet in which we preserve the national state and its attendant virtues at the cost of quite a small amount of international organization. If this were clearly perceived, many of the resistances to a more rational and inexpensive organization of the international system might be overcome. This indeed I regard as one of the great tasks of the next generation.

4

**Social Science and the
Sacred Aspects of Life**

In the two previous chapters, I used economic life
to illustrate an area where the social sciences have
had considerable impact and some success, and the
international system as the area where, perhaps, it
has had the least impact and the least success. In this
chapter I want to examine an area where the impact
of the social sciences is highly ambiguous, where there
is little doubt that some impact is taking place but
where it is not at all easy to evaluate the nature of this
impact or what the future holds for it. The area which
I particularly propose to examine might be called that
of the sacred aspects of life, which are characterized
by strong emotive affect, considerable reliance on authority, experiences which are in some sense out of

the ordinary and in which there is a considerable appeal to sanctions and authorities which are beyond the ordinary course of human experience. Three areas of social life which are markedly affected by the sacred interest are the law, religion, and ethics. Aesthetics and politics, marriage, the family, sex, death, art, architecture, and many other aspects of human life are likewise involved in sacredness. Limitations of space, however, forbid my giving these more than a scant mention.

We may begin with some rather cursory observations on the possible impact of the social sciences on the institutions of the law and the legal system. It may seem a little odd to put the law in the realm of the sacred, and certainly many aspects of it are concerned with very humdrum dealings—the making of wills, the drawing up of documents, the transfer of property, and so on. Nevertheless, the majesty of the law—and it has a majesty—is essentially sacred. The architecture of the courtroom, the robes of the judge, the ritual of the court, even the use of religious symbols, for instance in giving oaths, all point to certain aspects of the institution of the law which at least have the flavor of sacredness. The courtroom is more like a church than it is like a workshop or a department store, and its proceedings are devised to give its practitioners, its clients, and its victims a certain sense of superhuman authority and rectitude. Solemnity is one of the marks of the sacred, and it certainly characterizes the institutions and the practice of the law.

By contrast, science is not very sacred, even though it has its sacred moments and aspects, like nearly everything else. The white coat of the scientist is designed just to keep stains off his clothes, not to impress anybody with his majesty, even though in the hands of the drug advertisers it is occasionally used for that end. The authority of science is supposed to be the authority of fulfilled prediction, not the authority of the authorities or of the past. The atmosphere of a laboratory or of a computer room is more like that of a factory or a boiler room than it is like the attitude of a courtroom or a church. The question has been asked, therefore, whether science is not in some sense corrosive of sacred values and sacred institutions and becomes a substitute for them. One could even ask the question as to whether the social sciences will not in the long run become a substitute for the law. My broad personal answer to this question, and it is no more than a personal answer, is that I suspect that the sciences in general and the social sciences in particular are both substitutes and complements to the sacred aspects of life, and that whereas at some points they compete, at other points they reinforce, so that the over-all effect is ambiguous and very hard to determine.

At some points there is strong latent competition between the methods and results of the social sciences and the methods and results of the law, as reflected particularly in the attitudes of the subcultures towards the problem of information and knowledge. In the law, the assumption is generally made that if we want to know something, the thing to do is to find out who knows it and ask him, under penalties of perjury. This is the principle of the witness. The ritual of the court-room then centers a good deal around procedures to divine whether what the witness has said is true. Where there is conflict among witnesses, the procedure is designed to resolve the conflict by a hierarchical decision. The jury system is based on the proposition that what twelve good men and true agree about must also be true. The division of labor between the jury and the judge in which the jury decides on the guilt or innocence of the party and the judge pronounces the sentence is reminiscent of the proposition that whereas facts are human, values are divine.

The atmosphere of the social sciences is very different. Here the assumption tends to be made that if we are ignorant, it is not because the person who knows what needs to be known has yet to be found and put into the witness box; rather it is that nobody knows what needs to be known. If nobody knows what needs to be known, obviously he cannot be found and put in a witness box and asked. This is the funda-mental difference between the principle of the legal trial and the principle of research. About the closest the law gets to the concept of research is in the idea of the expert witness. Even here, however, it is the authority of the expert which gives him credibility rather than his capacity to make predictions which come true, and the ability of the law to produce contradictory experts on both sides of a question is notorious.

Up to now at any rate, the conflict between the law and the social sciences has been largely latent. Criminologists have been critical of certain aspects of the legal process, and have indeed succeeded in achieving certain reforms in it. Something, certainly, of the decline in the ferocity of the law and in the nature of its punishments has been due to doubts which the social sciences have raised in regard to the deterrent effect of punishment and its strong inferiority to reward as an incentive for learning. There is a strong undercurrent of protest against the prevailing attempts on the part of the law to deal with such matters as drug addiction and sexual deviation. Economists are apt to sneer at the simple-mindedness of the antitrust

laws, and they have certainly created enough confusion in the minds of the lawyers so that the antitrust
operation is strongly reminiscent of the man who got
up on a big white horse and rode off in all directions.
Nevertheless the conflicts are at the margins, and at
the moment at any rate the social sciences present
neither any serious challenge to the machinery of the
law nor any substitute for it. In the more enlightened
law schools, indeed, there is a great deal of interest in
utilizing the methods and the findings of the social
sciences in an evaluation of the effects of law and in
the improvement of its procedures. In an optimistic
mood, therefore, one may regard the two branches of
the knowledge profession as fundamentally comple-
mentary rather than in conflict.

It may be, however, that the absence of conflict is
simply a result of the smallness and weakness of the
social sciences by contrast with the high status, rewards, and prestige of the law. In the United States
at any rate, a Supreme Court justice has a status in the
eyes of the average man several orders of magnitude
above that of a sociologist, and the social scientist
is apt to look much more like a servant to the court
than a threat to it. It may be also that the potential
conflict between the law and the social sciences will
be mitigated and mediated by the development of
what one might call paralegal institutions, such as

arbitration, mediation and conciliation, marriage counseling, social work, and the like. The status of the
social-work profession is peculiar interest in this regard. It tends to become rather divorced from the
social sciences which gave rise to it, and the relation-
ship today, for instance, between sociology and social
work is distinctly cool. It may be, therefore, that the
development of intermediate professions between the
law and the social sciences is not a wholly satisfactory
solution, but still it is one we are quite likely to see
more of in the future. At the other end of the scale,
there is a certain feeling among the more conservative
and legalistic members of the legal profession that the
United States Supreme Court, for instance, is too much
influenced in its judgments by social-scientific or other
extralegal considerations, and one could well visualize
a conservative rebellion with the object of getting
the law back to legality. At the moment, therefore, the
ambiguity of the relations between the law and the
social sciences is very pronounced, and it is very hard
to predict which way things will go in the future.
Certainly it is by no means impossible that the kind
of accommodations which have been made hitherto
will continue and that serious conflict will be avoided.
On the other hand, it also seems to me within the
bounds of possibility that within the next couple of
generations, shall we say, as the social sciences acquire

strength and numbers, if accommodation does not proceed and if an increasing dissatisfaction with the "sacred" aspects of the law increases, a major social conflict might ensue, even though it might not be couched in such straightforward terms as the social sciences versus the law. It might take the form, for instance, of social-scientifically minded lawyers versus the more conservative and conventional types.

Religion is an aspect of the social system which might be described as specializing in the sacred. Like the law, it is embodied in an impressive panoply of institutions, that is, churches and religious societies. It represents a sizable slice of total human activity and interaction, and even though the religious impulse and experience is something which can be practiced in private its major social impact is in the form of church organizations. Religious institutions develop many functions in society, however, in addition to what might be thought of as their special functions in public worship and religious education. They are very important in the ethical system, in the sense that they establish and propagate certain norms of behavior and frequently invoke certain sacred sanctions against deviations from these norms, sanctions which may range all the way from the active terror of hell to a vague feeling of uneasiness with divine displeasure. The religious institution has an enormously important social function in the establishment of personal identity within the framework both of the small community of the congregation and also within the common culture of a larger group. The church congregation is an important supplement to the family in the training of children, the establishment of social norms, the provision of ideals and heroes, and the pro- vision of a community within which the individual may feel peculiarly at home. The church plays an important role in propagating an important part of the literary culture of the society. Thus the Bible or the Koran, the analects and the sutras in their respective cultures, provide a rich common reservoir of allusion and affective and emotive communication. The church organizes charity and expressions of social and com- munity concern both for its own members and for the community in which it lives. The church has a healing function, providing therapy for mental and spiritual distress and related disorders, and it does a good deal of informal counseling. It acts as a great agency of legitimation, not only in such obvious things as mar- riages and funerals, where it is used even by people who are not regularly in communion with it. Even in such matters as social reform the church can be used to give legitimacy to what otherwise would be regard- ed as a dangerous and rather illegitimate enterprise. The relations of the social sciences to the church are even more ambiguous than their relations to the law. One might expect to find a good deal of conflict. The atmosphere of the social sciences is very different from that of the church. Many social scientists, indeed, are refugees from the Sunday School and are personally quite hostile or at least ambivalent towards organized religion. One finds this particularly, perhaps, among the Jews, who have made contributions to the social sciences quite out of proportion to their numbers, perhaps because many of them find in the social sciences a substitute for the sense of social concern and concern for community which is characteristic of Judaic religion in all its forms, and yet which perhaps is imperfectly expressed in the organized synagogue. Social scientists likewise tend to be somewhat hostile to preaching, determined to avoid the deliberate propagation of values, and to a certain extent they find refuge in the formalities of the social sciences from the ambiguities of the religious organization.

Nevertheless, the conflict between the social sciences and the religious establishment, to this point at any rate, has been muted. It has not been nearly as severe, for instance, as the conflict which arose in the nineteenth century between the biological sciences, in the shape of the theory of evolution, and the church, which is still reflected in the anti-evolutionary laws in some Southern states; nor is it as severe as the conflict between Galileo and the church in a still earlier day. It could be argued, of course, that just as the relative mildness of the conflict between the social sciences and the law is due to the weakness of the social sciences, the relatively mild nature of the conflict between social sciences and the church is due to the weakness of the church. This, however, is too simple an explanation. In the first place the church, at least in the United States, is by no means a weak institution. Indeed, one of the most striking phenomena in the history of the United States has been the rise of organized religion from a position of being a small minority at the time of the Revolution and only 18 per cent of the population in the middle of the nineteenth century to its position today, with 64 per cent of the population in church membership; and the churches have very substantial political power.

The third main topic of this chapter, ethics, can be regarded as that segment of the total social system which deals with the learning of approved values and obligations through a complex system of human interaction in institutions of many kinds. Ethics as an aspect of the social system differs from the law and religion in that it is not defined sharply by a set of specialized institutions, and this makes it rather difficult to study. Nevertheless, a learning process can be identified by which people learn to distinguish between good and bad, right and wrong, approved and disapproved. This process takes place in the family, in the school, in the church, in the peer group, in face-to-face contacts of many kinds, in business, professional, academic, legal, and social life. There is, indeed, hardly any aspect of the system in which ethical values and obligations are not learned and even taught. In all parts of the system, however, the processes by which ethical norms are established have a degree of similarity. There are types of statements, arguments, communications, conversations, which can be readily identified as affected with the ethical interest. As a result of this, the norms of individuals in the subculture tend to come together and the norms of people in different cultures possibly tend to diverge. We can think of the ethical system, in fact, as a set of intersecting subcultures within which ethical communications are strong and tend to move the ethical positions of individuals towards a central norm, with increasing circles of diminishing intensity of communication, community, and commonality of ethical judgment.

Up to the present the ethical system has been almost universally part of the folk culture, with considerable overtones and inputs from the literary culture, in the shape of sacred documents like the Ten Commandments, the Sermon on the Mount, or perhaps even the Gettysburg Address, and in the shape also of a large collection of aphorisms, proverbs, well-known poems, hymns, and so on, which form, as it were, the linguistic memory bank of an ethical system. Up to now the social sciences have made very little impact on the ethical system. In some quarters, indeed, there is a strong tendency to deny that the social sciences can or should have *any* impact on it. Even so eminent and wise a figure as Don K. Price, for instance, argues that values are essentially given by the sacred processes of the folk and that scientists of all kinds, including the social scientist, should keep their stained fingers off.

Fortunately or unfortunately, this is a division of labor that cannot ultimately be maintained. We cannot simply regard the values of the society as determined by one set of learning processes and its scientific learning processes as consisting of something wholly separate. It is not only that as science changes our view of the universe, the value system even of the folk and the literary culture has to change to accommodate to this new view. The position of the social sciences is also of particular significance because it occupies the same field of the production of knowledge about social systems, human relations, and man himself that the ethical system occupies. It would be very surprising, therefore, if there were not substantial interactions between the two systems.

In spite of the very tenuous or even ambiguous relationships between the social sciences and the various aspects of the "sacred system," legal, ethical, and religious, the fact that their fields overlap forces them into contact. In the first place, legal, ethical, and religious systems are legitmate objects of study for the social scientists, and social scientists are exhibiting increasing interest in them. Insofar as the legal, religious, and ethical aspects of society are the principal components of what I have earlier called the "integrative system" by which we learn to establish such relationships as status, respect, community, legitimacy, affection, and so on, they are not merely legitimate objects of study for the social sciences but absolutely necessary ones without which none of the other social systems can be understood. Studying society without also studying law, religion, and ethics would be performing Hamlet without the Prince of Denmark. The institutions of both exchange and threat systems, for instance, must be legitimated if they are to be effective in organizing the role structure of society. I have come to believe, indeed, that the dynamics of legitimacy is perhaps the most fundamental force in all social systems, in the sense that the loss of legitimacy represents a total loss of the ability to organize. The dynamics of the gain and loss of legitimacy, however, is very little understood. It is clearly related to the sacred aspects of society. The law and the church, for instance, are two of the great agents conferring legitimacy, so they certainly cannot escape study.

We cannot, however, study anything with the instruments of the social sciences without changing our images of it. Insofar as the legal, ethical, and religious systems in the past have operated mainly with folk and literary images, the introduction of social-scientific images is bound to have a profound effect which may be either creative or disorganizing, depending in considerable degree on how it is received and what adjustments are made to it. It is not merely that there may be changes in institutions. There is likely to be an impact on the very ethical norms of the system, even though this impact is likely to be diffuse, since the ethical system itself is so diffuse. Even here, however, we can already detect a substantial impact. The power of an ethical norm is a very complex function of its conformity with the existing value structure of the society, perhaps with some abstract ethical truth, and with the perception of the extent to which the norm is in fact obeyed. Hence knowledge about the extent to which norms are in fact obeyed may have a substantial impact on the degree to which the norms are accepted. There may be, of course, norms which everybody accepts and nobody obeys, which still persist because of the other reasons for the persistence of norms. Nevertheless, if everybody knows that nobody obeys a particular norm, this is almost bound to undermine it. If something which is denounced from the pulpit or in the press is discovered to be a practice of a large proportion of the people, including perhaps even those who denounce it, the denunciations lose something of their effect. One could give innumerable examples of the impact of the social sciences on ethical norms, and a few specimens will have to suffice by way of illustration. National income economics, for instance, has called into question some of the ethical norms of the Puritan tradition which are still highly characteristic of the Far Right. What might be called the Puritan attitudes towards the national debt or towards government expenditure in general, or even towards private thriftiness, are called into serious question by a more sophisticated knowledge of economics. The profound ethical questions which are involved in, shall we say, the Marxist theory of surplus value, or the attack on economic rent, or the attack on private property in general, may be considerably modified in the light of knowledge about economic development. Success in development, indeed, makes the problem of distributional justice much less acute. When there is more for everybody, we don't have to worry so much about redistribution.

To turn to another field that may be even more

important, the impact of child-development psychologists such as Piaget and Gesell has had an enormous impact on the norms of child-rearing, and indeed on the character of the whole society. The folk knowledge of "spare the rod and spoil the child," which led to the perpetuation of such an enormous amount of unhappy childhood from generation to generation, now at least has moved to a more literary and scientific scale, with a generation raised on Dr. Spock, though we should probably be modest in our estimate of what we really know in this area, especially from the point of view of its long-run effects. We have already discussed the impact of the social sciences on the norms of the law and the shift from a punitive penology towards one which seeks, at any rate, to integrate the offender into the society, even though here again we may not be too proud of our success. Even in the matter of sexual ethics, the work of Dr. Kinsey (incidentally a biologist), by revealing the widespread character of certain practices which are ordinarily regarded as "abnormal," may lead to the re-evaluation of their abnormality, though not necessarily to the establishment of a totally new canon of legitimacy.

The accommodations of religion to scientific images of the universe has already been profound in the last three hundred years. It is interesting to observe, however, the extraordinary extent to which the content of the sacred is almost by definition screened from criticism by empirical testing. We see a nice example of this, for instance, in the Roman Catholic doctrine of the transubstantiation, in which it is insisted that it is the substance, not the accidents—that is, the physical properties—of the bread and wine which are changed in the mass and that hence the doctrine is quite incapable of being tested by physical or chemical analysis. Similarly, the acceptance or rejection of any particular sacred history is something which no amount of historical criticism seems to affect.

Insofar as ethical and religious systems, however, involve certain beliefs about the nature of social systems, they are subject to criticism from the social sciences, and this feedback may have profound consequences. A good example of this would be the shift in the emphases and nature of at least parts of the temperance movement as a result of social research into alcoholism. The shift from the prohibition movement to Alcoholics Anonymous, for instance, represents a real change in the image of the social system. It is hard not to feel that this is a change for the better and that the prohibition movement had a very narrow and unrealistic image of the nature of the social system, which led the movement to real disaster, from its own point of view. If there had been a more subtle realization of the interaction between all parts of the system of cultural norms a more realistic approach to the problem might have been possible. The greater sophistication of the civil-rights movement of the sixties, by comparison with the prohibition movement of the twenties, is an interesting example, not perhaps of the impact of social-science images as such, but of the general spread of more sophisticated images of social change in the society in the course of a couple of generations.

The deep ambiguity in the impact of the social sciences on religious institutions may be seen if we consider the fact that where these institutions have specific objectives in terms of social change or even of change in the personality of the individual, the social sciences can unquestionably be of assistance in developing an information process by which success in the achievement of these objectives is measured. Social-scientific studies of organization likewise suggest all sorts of ways in which the organization even of churches can be improved; and one could very well visualize a large number of ways in which the social sciences could be helpful in small ways in the achievement of given goals. In the course of doing this, however, the goals themselves may be called into question. This may well be perceived as being deeply threatening. Thus if we find, as Professor Rokeach does, that church members differ very little in their moral atti-

tudes from non-church members on a wide variety
of moral norms, this at least raises an important question about the efficacy of moral training in the church,
and it may even call into question certain fundamental
values which up to now have been unquestioned in
the culture of the church. One of the sources of legitimacy in any society is that the legitimate is simply
not called into question. The moment an ancient legitimacy is called into question it is often very deeply
threatened, simply because where legitimacy depends
on something not being questioned, the very asking
of a question threatens it in a way that cannot be
answered with any answer. The only answer to asking
the question is, don't ask the question; and this is
one thing that in a social-science culture is illegitimate.

We see the same phenomenon perhaps even more
acutely in the impact of science and social sciences
on national culture and national legitimacies. If social
science comes up with the answer that the national
state is obsolete and dangerous and should be done
away with, all sorts of ancient legitimacies and values
are deeply threatened, and we would certainly not be
surprised to see extreme conflict as a result. There is
no guarantee whatever, therefore, that the pursuit of
the subculture of the social sciences will not result
in some deep conflicts with the fundamental values of
other subcultures within the society. It is hard to pre-

vent truth from having consequences, and these consequences are not necessarily pleasant.

Nevertheless, a mild optimism can at least be indulged in without absurdity. In the developed world at least, the sacred systems seem to have shown themselves capable of quite remarkable adaptability to the impact of the sciences. We have seen an unusually spectacular example of this in the remarkable changes which have taken place in the last few years in the Roman Catholic Church, in the way of "aggiornamento." While, therefore, the impact of the social sciences on the sacred systems of society is ambiguous and uncertain, a modest optimism suggests that the results will not be catastrophic, that the sacred system will adjust to new knowledge and new images of the social world, and that even the social sciences themselves may come to accept the sacred as an essential element of the social system which they do not necessarily have to fight and from which they may even derive some legitimation and benefit.

Far from science and the social sciences being the instrumental handmaids of a previously established folk value system, we may find that the most useful product of the social sciences turns out to be a critique of value systems themselves, something which might redound enormously to the benefit of mankind. As one

looks over human history it is hard to avoid the conclusion that there are diseases of the value system,
and that while these may not be as easy to identify
as the diseases of the body, they are certainly equally
real and perhaps have caused even more misery. It
may well be that peaceful coexistence, or maybe even
better, peaceful cooperation, between the social sciences and the sacred aspects of social life will develop
a therapy for values and prevent at least the worst
excesses in terms of false heroics, self-justified malev-
olence, and narrow-minded nationalisms and sectar-
ianisms which have so afflicted mankind.

At this point, however, the modesty of our optimism
should at least be equaled by the modesty of our pride.
The plain fact is that in those aspects of the social
system which are most relevant to the sacred aspects
of life in society, the social sciences really know very
little. The sacred systems, whether of the law, religion,
or ethics, are deeply involved in what might be called
the "symbolic" systems of society, and this as social
scientists we know very little about. We do not know
what it is, for instance, that gives certain symbols an
enormous appeal and power at certain times and places
and virtually no appeal and power at other times and
places. Symbols such as the Cross, the Virgin, the
Crescent, the flag, even surplus value, have moved

mountains and created enormous organizations and movements of men, yet we really do not understand why this is so. As the honest social scientist studies history, he is constantly led to ejaculate, "Who could have known!"

Who could have known, for instance, that a carpenter at an obscure town in a tiny province of the Roman Empire would have established a movement that was going to build enormous cathedrals in countries and continents the Romans never heard of? Who would have thought that a charismatic camel driver in the middle of Arabia a few hundred years later would have established a movement that led to a great civilization stretching from Spain to the Philippines, on the edge of which Christian Europe in the Middle Ages was a troublesome, barbaric peninsula? Who would have thought that an irascible old man with a beard in the British Museum in the middle of the nineteenth century would have fired the imagination of a third of the human race in the next hundred years? For all we know, the most important thing that is happening today is happening in an obscure valley in Ethiopia or Afghanistan and we will not even learn about it for fifty years.

It is reflections like this that make the social scientist pause when he comes to attempt prediction, especially in the sacred system. The fact is that we know very little about what it is that moves great masses of men to action, and until we know more about this it is fitting for the social scientist to maintain a becoming modesty in the presence of a great deal to be modest about.

5

✿✿✿✿ **The Impact of the Social System
on the Social Sciences:
A Brief Epilogue**

It is essential to the understanding of the relations
between the social sciences and the social system to
realize that the social sciences are themselves part
of the social system and are produced by it. It is of
the nature of knowledge processes and evolutionary
systems that they feed on themselves and that each
part feeds back into the other with positive or at least
disequilibrating feedback.

In the previous chapters we have looked at some
of the present and potential impacts of the social sciences on society. The total system, however, is cir-
cular, and a society itself has an enormous impact on
the social sciences. The food of science is the interests
and curiosity of the scientist and the interests and

curiosities of the people who support him. Interests and curiosity are rarely entirely idle, even though the role of idle curiosity in the system, simply because it is as it were fed into the system from outside, has an impact which is quite disproportionate to its quantity. But non-idle curiosity is that which arises out of a perception of the salient problems of the system, for it is only when problems become salient and enter the conscious awareness that conscious intellectual resources are devoted to their solution.

We should expect, therefore, to find that as the dynamics of the social system bring one or another problem to salient positions, the interests of the social sciences change accordingly. The social sciences themselves are part of the social system, and what is salient in the system is apt to be salient to them. An even more important reason, perhaps, is that the people who support social sciences are also salient in the system, and the pressure for the solution of salient problems therefore comes from "he who pays the piper." It is not surprising that the tunes are a function of the age.

Thus in the eighteenth century, when trade was expanding on a world scale, when exchange was turning out to be enormously important as a social organizer, and when government restrictions were generally perceived as hampering, Adam Smith came up with a doctrine of natural liberty, the theory of the divison of labor, and development through free exchange and free markets. Malthus, as we noted, seemed to be ahead of his time, though influential for all that. It is easy to see in Marx and Engels a reaction to the feudal Germany of the time, to the "hungry forties" and the conditions of paleo-industrial Manchester. Similarly, Keynes is clearly a response to the Great Depression and to the apparently meaningless and bewildering experience of large-scale unemployment in a relatively developed society. The interest in economic development of the last generation is clearly inspired by the saliency and difficulty of the problem, especially in the tropical countries. Then too, the collapse of the old system of unilateral national defense has inspired a great deal of system-building and the beginning of serious and empirical work in the field of the international system.

It is perhaps worth while, therefore, taking a somewhat speculative glance at the future, to ask ourselves what are likely to be the salient problems in the social systems of the future and how are these likely to affect the social sciences. It is hard, indeed, not to be impressed today with an extraordinary misallocation of intellectual resources, in the sense that these resources are simply not employed in the major fields where the problems lie. Thus within the professions we find that the greatest prestige and frequently the greatest rewards go to professions such as law, medicine, and engineering, with social work and education about at the bottom of the list.

Yet law is concerned mainly with the redistribution of old rights and properties, and surely if it were staffed with considerably less able minds than it is now society would be very little worse off. Medicine is devoting itself increasingly to keeping sick old people alive and, together with the health sciences, has on the whole achieved its current mission of extending the average age of death to the allotted span of seventy years. Anything beyond this is still for the future and may be of very doubtful desirability. Engineers, because of their insensitivity to the importance of social systems, are constantly devoting their lives to finding out the best way of doing something which should not be done at all. Planning that is done by engineers in the absence of any conscious appreciation of the social system within which it operates is frequently disastrous. One could cite water policy, flood control, urban renewal, highway construction, and a good many other cases in which physical planning turns out to be socially costly. There are only two or three thousand sociologists in the whole country, most of them engaged in teaching. The practical research in social systems which is necessary at all levels of decision-making, both public and private, is simply not being done, partly because of the sheer absence of people to do it, partly because of a failure to understand that this is what is needed.

Even within the social sciences themselves one finds a distressing lack of correspondence between the resources devoted to problems and the intensity and importance of the problems. This maldistribution is particularly flagrant in economics, where, for instance, we have an enormous intellectual resource going into agricultural economics when agriculture is only 5 per cent of the gross national product, while educational economics is virtually non-existent, urban economics is very scantily supported, and even transportation economics is a rare specialty. In recent years there has been some good work done in the economics of the household, but even here far less than the intrinsic importance of the subject requires. Now that the war industry is some 10 per cent of the GNP there has been a belated rise of interest in the economics of it, but there has been astonishingly little interest in the economics of imperialism, of coexistence, of land ownership, and many other aspects of the world which seem to me at any rate very crucial.

In sociology the situation is not much better. Research in race relations virtually ceased with the Supreme Court decision of 1954, and one can find even quite large sociology departments with nobody

working in this field in spite of its enormous importance. Criminology has received extraordinarily little
attention from the theorists and even the statisticians
in the last generation, and one might almost describe it
as a stagnant field. The sociology of the family has
been shockingly neglected in recent years after some
very exciting work a generation ago. The sociology
of education is a largely uncultivated field. There is
a huge area of economic sociology—the sociology of
markets, the financial system, the banking system, the
Federal Reserve system, the budget-making processes
in all organizations and government, the corpora-
tion—all of which is virtually virgin territory. In part
this reflects the small size of the profession itself, in
part it reflects perhaps a movement, as in economics,
towards the easier payoffs.

Psychology is such a heterogeneous discipline—one
might almost describe it as a loose federation of virtually unrelated enterprises—that it is harder to specify
where the untilled fields lie. Perhaps there are fewer
of them than in the other social sciences. I am struck,
however, with the relatively meager resource which
is devoted to the problem of human learning, in spite
of the fact that this is the core of virtually all developmental processes. I am also struck with the absence
of treatment of such phenomena as the psychology of
nationalism, the study of political mental ill health,

the psychological impact of advertising or television, and so on.

Anthropology is the aristocrat of the social sciences, and is perhaps the least open to the criticism of intellectual misapplication, though it can be criticized on the grounds of its aloofness from the other social sciences and its unwillingness to learn from them, especially in regard to economic organization.

Turning now to the borderline disciplines between the social sciences and humanities, such as history and geography, one finds a striking contrast. Geography is in a state of great intellectual ferment, busy absorbing new methods, especially quantitative methods, on all sides, and quite self-consciously aware of its role as an integrator of many social sciences and natural sciences besides. Of all the disciplines, geography is the one that has caught the vision of the study of the earth as a total system, and it has strong claims to be the queen of the human sciences.

By contrast, history, which should be simply the geography of time, has reacted so strongly against the speculative and philosophical theories of those who might be called the naïve or premature synthesizers like Marx, Spengler, and Toynbee, that the historians seem almost to have retreated into the trivial and to be terrified of anything that looks like a generalization. There are some small welcome signs of change, especially among the younger men, some of whom are beginning to get interested in the application of social-systems theory to historical data, but this at times looks like a rather small straw in a very faint breeze.

If there is a misallocation of intellectual resources, as I claim, this must be a product of the social system itself, and it should be possible to identify at least some of the elements which are responsible for it. The critic may say: "Who are you to pit yourself against the wisdom of society, and to say that the existing allocation of resources is not ideal? After all, it is the social system that has thrown up this allocation, and who are you to criticize it?" The only answer to this is to show with some detail what processes in the social system are likely to throw up a misallocation of intellectual resources and to show that these processes operate in our own social system. The social system itself must be called to witness to our own lack of understanding of it.

I claim, then, that there are three processes which are at work in all social systems, and particularly in our own, to pervert the allocation of resources, especially intellectual resources.

The first of these is what I have elsewhere called "Richardson processes" because they were first developed by Lewis Richardson in his classic work on *Arms and Insecurity*. These are highly similar to the processes which are described in the famous "Prisoner's Dilemma" game. They are the processes present in arms races, price wars, and what might be described as self-justifying and unproductive emulation.

The misallocation of resources into the law is a good example of this. In legal situations, one lawyer is pitted against another. Under these circumstances, the dynamics of the system means that for any individual person there is a payoff in having the best lawyer. Under these circumstances it is not surprising that the law attracts some of the ablest minds of our society and that the payoffs for high ability are probably as great in the law as in any other profession if not greater. If, however, we could achieve a kind of intellectual disarmament and agree that nobody would be allowed in the legal profession with an IQ above a hundred, the result would be almost exactly similar; people would still try to buy the best lawyers they could, but a valuable intellectual resource would be economized.

The grotesque waste of resources which is represented by the world war industry, $120 billion a year or more, is a similar testimony to the misallocating impact of Richardson processes. Just as the client wants the best lawyer, a nation wants the best armed force. This results in an enormous waste of intelligence devoted to the means of destruction or the threat of destruction. Here again it would require a high level of organization to achieve stable peace and disarmament, but simply because this *does* represent a higher level of organization, the existing system must be condemned as a misallocation.

The second reason for the misallocation of intellectual resources is an old friend called lag. The phenomenon of cultural lag has been noticed for a long time. Social systems, like all other systems, have momentum. They tend to continue, that is, long after the initial force which gave rise to them has disappeared. The misallocation of resources into agriculture is a clear case in point. In the days when agriculture was 50 per cent of the economy, a large allocation made an enormous amount of sense; today, with agriculture only 5 per cent of the gross national product, it seems clear that we could divert a large part of the intellectual resource that now goes into agricultural research into other fields. The momentum persists, however, in the agricultural colleges, the departments of agricultural economics, the United States Department of Agriculture, enormous institutional vested interests the purpose for which has largely passed away. In another generation or two we may catch up with this and begin to divert some of these resources; in the meantime, momentum carries us forward.

The third source of misallocation of intellectual resources might be described as a spurious or intrinsic saliency. Out of innumerable studies of human behavior, even of such supposedly rational things as business behavior, an important principle emerges. This principle is that some events are intrinsically more salient than others, that is they make a deeper impression on the human mind, quite apart from their role in the over-all system. A few miners entombed in a mine arouse the pity and agony of the whole world and produce headlines everywhere; forty thousand people a year slaughtered on the roads produce no corresponding response.

There seem to be events which are intrinsically dramatic, and these pre-empt our attention, even though in quantitative terms they may be a small part of the total system. As the proverb says, it is the squeaky wheel that gets the grease. Noisy and troublesome people get attention; the quiet are ignored, even when they are wise. This again explains in part why the lawyer and the soldier and the surgeon, involved as they are in dramatic events even though they may be of small importance, occupy salient positions in the system, whereas the classroom teacher, the harassed mother, and the social worker, on whose ill-rewarded and often rather inept hands the future of the society rests, are regarded as boring and attract no attention. It is always easier to get people to pursue the interesting than the important. The critic might again say, who am I to say that the interesting is not important? And again he has a point, especially if the consumer is always right. Nevertheless, a false saliency is clearly something against which one can take precautions.

The social sciences themselves, interestingly enough, have become a very important agency in the devaluing of the spectacular and the spuriously salient and through sampling techniques have emphasized the importance of obtaining well-sampled knowledge of a total system. Even in pursuing their own objectives, however, the social sciences do not follow their own principles, and the problem of spurious saliency continually arises. It arises not only in the interests of the social scientists themselves, who tend to be attracted to what seems exciting at the moment, but also because scientific research of all kinds is largely supported by the grants economy. Grantors, whether governments or foundations or even patrons, the concerned and interesting rich, are subject to fashions, fads, and enthusiasms and certainly do not prepare the allocation of their resources by any careful sampling of the problems involved.

In the light of these three elements in the social system, the tendency towards misallocation seems to me hardly open to question, and the problem is, what can be done about it. What I have done about it is to write this book, in the endeavour to make the problem of saliency salient. Once a problem has been perceived, the arts of rhetoric ought to be called into play to make it salient. To these arts of rhetoric I recommend my fellow social scientists, however distasteful this may be to them. To those of my listeners and readers who are not social scientists, I recommend careful attention, a listening ear, and a modicum of loving care towards those who are struggling, however imperfectly, to understand the delicate intricacies of the social system. Attend to them carefully, though not blindly. The social system you save may be your own,

✿✿✿✿ References

PAGE

24 Smith, Adam, *Inquiry into the Nature and Causes of the Wealth of Nations* (1776). Cannan's edition (London: Methuen, 1904) is probably the best. This has been republished in the Modern Library, New York.

25 Ricardo, David, *Principles of Political Economy and Taxation* (1817), is available in Everyman's Library, New York.

26 Malthus, T. R., *Essay on Population* (1798) is in Everyman's Library, New York, and also in Ann Arbor Paper Books, Ann Arbor, Michigan.

32 Marx, Karl, *Das Kapital* (1867). The translation by Eden and Cedar Paul (London: Allen and Unwin, 1928) is very good; the Modern Library edition, New York, containing Stephen Trask's translation of Borchardt's condensation together with *The Communist Manifesto*, is an excellent introduction.

PAGE

36 Keynes, J. M.: his major works are the *Treatise on Money* (New York: Harcourt, Brace, 1931) and the *General Theory of Employment, Interest, and Money* (New York: Harcourt, Brace, 1936).

37 Cournot, A. A., *Recherches sur les principes mathématiques de la théorie des richesses* (1838), English translation by N. T. Bacon (New York: Macmillan, 1897).
Walras, Léon, *Eléments d'économie politique pure* (4th ed., Lausanne, 1900), English translation by William Jaffé, *Elements of Pure Economics* (London: Irwin, 1954).
Pareto, V., *Cours d'économie politique* (Lausanne, 1896); *Manuale di economia politica* (Milan, 1906).
Mitchell, Wesley: his last work, *What Happens During Business Cycles* (New York: National Bureau of Economic Research, 1951), is probably the best introduction.

50 Hagen, Everett E., *On the Theory of Social Change* (Homewood, Ill.: Dorsey Press, 1962).
McClelland, David C., *The Achieving Society* (Princeton, N. J.: Van Nostrand, 1961).

63 Snow, C. P., *The Two Cultures and the Scientific Revolution* (New York: Cambridge University Press, 1959).

69 Richardson, Lewis, *Arms and Insecurity* and *Statistics of Deadly Quarrels* (Pittsburgh: Boxwood Press, 1960).
Wright, Quincy, *A Study of War*, abridged edition (Chicago: University of Chicago Press, 1964).
Schelling, Thomas C., *The Strategy of Conflict* (Cambridge: Harvard University Press, 1960).
Deutsch, Karl W., *Nationalism and Social Communication* (Cambridge: Technology Press of M. I. T., 1953).

70 Singer, David, *Deterrence, Arms Control, and Disarmament* (Columbus, O.: Ohio State University Press, 1962).

PAGE

70 McClelland, Charles A., *Theory and the International System* (New York: Macmillan, 1966).

Robert North is Director of the Studies in International Conflict and Integration at Stanford University.

Kaplan, Morton, *System and Process in International Politics* (New York: Wiley, 1957).

Boulding, K. E., *Conflict and Defense* (New York: Harper and Bros., 1962 and 1963).

94 Piaget, Jean, *The Child's Conception of the World* (New York: Harcourt, Brace, 1929), followed by many other volumes on related topics.

Gesell, Arnold, and Frances Ilg, *Child Development, an Introduction to the Study of Human Growth* (New York: Harper and Bros., 1949).

Spock, Benjamin M., *Common Sense Book of Baby and Child Care* (New York: Duell, Sloan and Pearce, 1946).

Kinsey, Alfred C., *Sexual Behavior in the Human Male* (Philadelphia: Saunders, 1948) and *Sexual Behavior in the Human Female* (Philadelphia: Saunders, 1953).

108 Spengler, Oswald, *The Decline of the West*, translated by C. F. Atkinson (New York: Knopf, 1926-1928).

Toynbee, Arnold J., *A Study of History* (9 vols.; London: Oxford University Press, 1934, reprinted as an Oxford Galaxy Paperback, New York: 1962).

110 Rapoport, Anatol, and A. Chammah, *Prisoner's Dilemma: A Study in Conflict and Cooperation* (Ann Arbor: University of Michigan Press, 1965).

✿✿✿✿ **About the Author**

Kenneth E. Boulding, professor and director of the program on general social and economic dynamics of the Institute of Behavioral Science of the University of Colorado since 1967, was born in Liverpool and educated at Oxford University. He has taught at a number of distinguished universities, was a Fellow at the Center for Advanced Study in the Behavioral Sciences in 1954–55, and was one of the founders of the Society for General Systems Research in 1957. Among his honors is the American Council of Learned Societies Prize for Distinguished Scholarship in the Humanities (1962). Mr. Boulding is the author of many articles and thirteen books, including *The Organizational Revolution* (1935), *The Image* (1956), *The Skills of the Economist* (1958), *Conflict and Defense* (1962), *The Meaning of the Twentieth Century* (1964), *Economic Analysis* (4th ed., 1965) and *Beyond Economics* (1968).